TO

_____

FROM

_____

DATE

_____

When We Talk to God

Prayers & Poems for Black Women

SHARIFA STEVENS

THOMAS NELSON

Since 1798

Published in Nashville, Tennessee, by Thomas Nelson. Thomas Nelson is a registered trademark of HarperCollins Christian Publishing, Inc.

Thomas Nelson titles may be purchased in bulk for educational, business, fund-raising, or sales promotional use. For information, please email SpecialMarkets@ThomasNelson.com.

Unless otherwise noted, Scripture quotations are from the Holy Bible, New International Version®, NIV®. Copyright © 1973, 1978, 1984, 2011 by Biblica, Inc.® Used by permission of Zondervan. All rights reserved worldwide. www.zondervan.com. The "NIV" and "New International Version" are trademarks registered in the United States Patent and Trademark Office by Biblica, Inc.®

Scripture quotations marked KJV are from the King James Version. Public domain.

Scripture quotations marked NASB are from the New American Standard Bible® (NASB). Copyright © 1960, 1962, 1963, 1968, 1971, 1972, 1973, 1975, 1977, 1995 by The Lockman Foundation. Used by permission. www.Lockman.org

Any internet addresses, phone numbers, or company or product information printed in this book are offered as a resource and are not intended in any way to be or to imply an endorsement by Thomas Nelson, nor does Thomas Nelson vouch for the existence, content, or services of these sites, phone numbers, companies, or products beyond the life of this book.

Note: The views and opinions expressed in this book are those of the author and do not necessarily reflect those of the publisher.

Cover art and interior illustrations: Camilla Ru
Art direction: Tiffany Forrester
Interior design: Kristen Sasamoto
Photography credits: Lexi Meadows, page 165; Camilla Ru, page 166

ISBN 978-1-4002-4968-8 (HC)
ISBN 978-1-4002-4967-1 (audiobook)
ISBN 978-1-4002-4969-5 (eBook)

Printed in Malaysia

25 26 27 28 29 COS 10 9 8 7 6 5 4 3 2 1

This book is for
Mommy
Grandma
Aunt Shirley
Aunt Mae
Aunt Georgia
Joanne
Rhea
Kim
Tiffany
Your lives are the melody that surrounds me.
I learned to sing through the music of your care.

Contents

When We Talk to God About Our Protest

When We Talk to God About Our Loved Ones

When We Talk to God About Our Heartbreak

When We Talk to God About Our Joy

When We Talk to God About Our Faith

Introduction

Now I lay me down to sleep
I pray the Lord my soul to keep
If I should die before I wake
I pray the Lord my soul to take

Our Father, which art in heaven
Hallowed be thy name
Thy kingdom come
Thy will be done
In earth as it is in heaven
Give us this day our daily bread
And forgive us our debts
As we forgive our debtors
And lead us not into temptation
But deliver us from evil
For thine is the kingdom, and the power, and the glory
For ever
Amen[1]

These two prayers were the spiritual scaffolding for my prayer life. I memorized and recited them before I knew to slow down and ponder what I was asking God. Once I did, I had to make some changes. First, the nursery rhyme about dying in my sleep as a child went right into my mental trash bin along with the raggedy lullaby about babies in cradles falling from trees. And second, I got curious about prayer itself.

Who are we talking to when we pray? We're talking to God, yes, but not a distant deity. We are talking to our Father. If you happen to have an adoring, protective, wise father or father figure already, you have a sense of what this means. When we pray, we're speaking to the Father who loves us fiercely, who desires our good, who joyfully created us, and who always has time to hear from us.

Luxuriate in that truth for a moment: When you pray, the Father leans in to listen with attentive love.

Too many of us have been taught that God tolerates us only because Jesus died for us. In other words, the Father intended to murder us because of the stench of sin that clings to us. Because of Jesus' sacrifice, we have access to the triune God, but when we pray, our prayers still waft up like bad breath, unless we can achieve spiritual perfection, somehow, down here on earth.

Many of us were taught a lot of violent theology, which leads to fear.

There's no good news in a gospel of mere tolerance and distance. But if God is our loving Father, we are safe to talk to Him.

Who am I to write a book of prayers? This question recurred in my mind as I sat down to write this book for us. I struggled with feeling qualified. Yes, I love Jesus and I am a Black woman—and proud of both. Yes, I pray. Yes, I earned a master's in theology (as if theology is a thing to be mastered). These aspects certainly inform me.

My grandmother was qualified. When I was little, she lived with us, and for a time, I got to share a room with her. She tutored me in prayer by example: She sank slowly to her knees every morning and

> **When you pray, the Father leans in to listen with attentive love.**

night, Bible and hymnal spread out before her. What little space by the side of the bed she had, she used to talk to and sing to God. Watching her gave me such a sense of security; I knew there was one person in my life who knew God and talked to God about us. We were covered.

Her death broke me wide open. I felt like a tether to heaven had been cut. Who would stand in the breach for us? My grandmother's spiritual influence propelled me on a path to seminary and placed me squarely at the feet of Jesus. I would need, more than ever, to know Him for myself—to talk to Him directly.

The problem was I was *not* my grandmother. I tried to mimic her method of praying, but it didn't fit my mouth. I went to a seminary that taught about God as best they could. Unfortunately, they taught only select European expressions of Christianity, actively excluding the histories of everyone else—including the Black church, whose theology has survived enslavement and oppression and birthed the Civil Rights Movement. Even some of the brothers at the seminary attempted to put me in my place because I was a woman learning Greek and Hebrew alongside them; they viewed this as an attempt to usurp authority.

Before and during seminary, fear shepherded me. Instead of dining at the Good Shepherd's table of Psalm 23, I sat at fear's table, fraught with anxiety about failing my kin and my God. I had better excel in school, I had better save myself for marriage, I had better not question the Bible, and I had better not chat back. Crossing those lines meant crossing an unforgivable abyss, away from worth and salvation.

Vigilance and worry followed me, seemingly all the days of my life. Joyless pragmatism replaced abundance. Fear can't offer good news— just the next possible attack, or the threat of getting lost. It's a false gospel ruled by bad news. Being a sheep under the care of fear meant knowing, always, that I am prey. Step out of line and be devoured. I didn't want to talk much to this God I feared, though I wanted God's mercy. I devoted myself to rule-following and staying in line—being "good."

This "good" news never saves the girls who crossed the lines of good behavior—and there are so many lines. Those lines drew electric fences around my thoughts and movements, dictating my hems and necklines, confounding my curiosity about what it would be like to kiss someone, threatening me for feeling outrage and disgust while reading about Jephthah's daughter[2] and the Levite's concubine.[3]

I went so deep within myself to stay within those lines that I am still drawing myself out. To this day. To this day.

So much of my spiritual formation involved evasive measures and self-defense that my arms went numb sifting love and discipleship from benevolent misogyny. My hands tired of swatting prying hands from my curls, my breasts, or anything else that appealed as exotic to both men and women who bypassed my consent to touch. My back and neck got tired of shrinking to cosplay a docile Black woman in proper, quiet submission to God. This was no place for the weary or heavy-laden. *What is it like to be protected by a good shepherd? Why do shepherds feel the same as wolves? When is it safe to come out?*

I thought that fear was God. I thought that love was as horrifying as a crucifixion.

Through it all, the beauty of the Lord shone through. Sometimes I can hardly believe the difference between Jesus' table and the table of fear: God who is *with* us? God who feels at ease in the womb of a woman? God whose conversations with women showed no disdain or condescension? God who would rather die than lay waste? God who will not rape or assault me? What wondrous love is this?

This is the loving God who inclines an ear to listen to our cries—our fancy language doesn't matter. What matters is our honesty about our need. How do I know? I read it in the Bible: God heard the pain and pragmatism of Tamar, Rahab, Ruth, Bathsheba. They came to God just as they were. They handled the challenges of the world as best they could, and God was with them. That, to me, is good news.

> **Our fancy language doesn't matter. What matters is our honesty about our need.**

Tamar was a sexually exploited widow who snatched justice by posing as a prostitute.[4] Rahab was a Gentile sex worker (the Bible calls her "Rahab the Prostitute"[5] in the books of Joshua, Hebrews, and James) who saw the Lord more clearly than most of the Israelites, and she cut a pragmatic deal to save her family before Israel took the city of Jericho.[6] Ruth was also a foreigner to the Israelites, starving, and desperate to make a way for herself and her mother-in-law.[7] Bathsheba was exploited by a king while her husband fought the king's war.[8] These women prayed with everything they had: their words, their strategies, their rituals, and their faith. (You should absolutely read their testimonies in Genesis 38, Joshua 2, the book of Ruth, and 2 Samuel 11.)

These women—and more whom I haven't named—navigated life outside the center of society. They were women, some were foreign (in Hebrew, the word for "foreign woman"—*nokri*[9]—was also used to describe a prostitute, which shows how they were regarded), who held little power and who were vulnerable to a system that exploited them when it should have protected them.

Sound familiar?

When I was growing up, my best friend, Rhea, and I would often talk about cutting an album (*that* is how old I am) called *Invisible*

Woman, chronicling the heartaches of coming of age as a societal ghost—too often at the whim of a culture that saw right through us when it wasn't too busy being terrified of us. In that album, we would write, wail, rage, and moan about the conundrum of being both hypervisible and ignored as Black girls—the ways both chivalry and feminism seemed to skip over us when it came to boys, teachers, police, or church folk. We were too strong for the (white) feminist movement and too Black to be the European feminine ideal (or to be a video vixen, for that matter). We waded through men's catcalls during middle school and shoves and elbowing on the subway at any age.

> **We survived by talking to one another when the world told us to hush and be grateful in a hundred different ways.**

Our churches taught us that the highest virtue of Christianity for us was to be a "good girl": virginal, quiet, accommodating, modest. Good girls don't talk back. They submit. If we were good, we would reap the reward of being God's favorites, of attracting a good husband, and of cultivating a godly family and financially blessed home. We submitted ourselves in the name of the Lord. We tried to swallow the doctrines of holiness that separated us from our bodies, even as the larger culture vilified us for our hues and our lips, hips, butts, and thighs. We wore large, dark T-shirts in the pool. We secretly taped our favorite songs on the radio when we were forbidden to listen to worldly music.

We were trained to suck up indignities and breathe out calm, like Anita Hill testifying about Clarence Thomas's harassment before the senate[10] or Diamond Reynolds's pleading with the officer who shot her love, Philando Castile, in front of her and her child.[11] We learned to absorb trauma to survive. And we survived by talking to one another when the world told us to hush and be grateful in a hundred different ways.

We are coerced to exist with an unreasonable strength. Malcolm X described the Black woman in America as the most disrespected, the most unprotected, the most neglected.[12] Too often, with heightened strength and sustained vigilance, we navigate spaces where we are either regarded as threats or not regarded at all. This burdens us with constant stress, fatigue, illness.

I do not believe this is our portion.

This is what the Lord says:

"Come to me, all you who are weary and burdened, and I will give you rest. Take my yoke upon you and learn from me, for I am gentle and humble in heart, and you will find rest for your souls. For my yoke is easy and my burden is light." (Matthew 11:28–30)

God has a kingdom breaking into this earthly world. The kingdom is a place of flourishing, healing, worship, joy. Jesus' incarnation is a powerful part of this breaking in. He comes to say, "Good news! I have come to set you free from the garbage kingdom of this world and restore you to God!" Prayer is asking for that kingdom to break through—for God's will to be done—in areas of our world and lives that need healing from racism, sickness, estrangement, poverty, malice. Prayer is also celebrating the joyous breakthrough of love, friendship, provision, care.

I wrote this book because I want us to receive the rest and safety that Jesus offers. That is what makes me qualified to write this book. God is with me as I make sense of the world around me in this skin, with this body, in this society, at this time. God isn't looking for my perfection before being present with me—and the same is true for you.

Who we pray to matters. These prayers are Christian, written to address the triune God: one God, three persons—Father, Son, and Holy Spirit. Throughout the book, I will use different titles for God that relate to the subject matter of the prayer, and sometimes I'll address different persons in the Trinity, but at all times, I am referring to the Christian, triune God.

I use the pronoun "He" to describe God sometimes, but God is beyond a single pronoun. Women are also made in God's image, so it shouldn't be controversial that women also reflect God—*of course* God contains the feminine as well as the masculine! The Bible quotes Jesus comparing Himself to a mother hen[13] and to a woman looking for a lost coin.[14] The book of Isaiah associates God the Father with motherly instincts.[15] The Spirit, in both Hebrew (*ruah*) and Greek (*pneuma*), is either feminine or gender neutral.[16]

We have access to God's ear anytime, anywhere; we don't need to be in a church sanctuary to pray. During times of joy, accomplishment, and awe. During challenges, doubt, or loss. The choice to talk to God is an audacious act of faith. We speak, believing God is there—even through the pain. Honestly, we don't even need *words* to pray. The Holy Spirit can translate even our groans at times when words fail us.[17]

How to Use This Book

This book is written for Black women who want to talk to God but who might not have the energy to articulate their fear, or praise, or questions—at least at first. Consider these prayers a starting point, then continue the conversation in your own words.

Please put this book to work: Read through the table of contents, flip to prayers or poems that speak to your struggle or joy, scribble your own prayers in the margins. You don't have to read this book cover to cover in one sitting, but my hope is that you'll return to it during significant life events—to bless yourself or others, to articulate grief or anger, to express gratitude for the everyday joy the Lord has given you.

The pieces within the book are deeply personal to me and reflect the depth and variety of my lived experiences. You can expect some very unserious pieces, some broody ones, some angry ones. Some prayers and poems are communal, some are written in the first person. There's variety here—in length, in composition, in style. I took my cues for writing, tone, and subject from the Bible itself, which has both poetry and prose and includes psalms of anger, doubt, and thanksgiving; historical events, communal rituals, letters, and personal reflections; and even has a whole book on love and joyful sexual expression.

I hope this book empowers you to know you are a beloved daughter of the Lord. You have access to the throne room of God at any time for any reason. Consider this book a love letter. I want you, Black woman, sister, to see your cares articulated in the writing of this book and feel both prayed for and seen as you read through its pages.

> **I hope this book empowers you to know you are a beloved daughter of the Lord. You have access to the throne room of God.**

Why Write a Book of Prayers for Black Women?

Because we exist. And our joys and pains are worth articulating and praying through. Because the truth is we don't earn God's favor; we are born into it, and favor ain't fair (hallelujah). And because the impossible effort of being a good girl stunts our growth. Good "girls" don't get to grow into women. They cannot speak on sexual satisfaction, or abuse, or their own volition. Good girls cannot be prodigal. They cannot wander; they must stay put and obey. They cannot leave and ever hope to be welcomed back home. But God created us to grow. God is not intimidated by a grown woman, and our gracious God does welcome us back home.

I also wrote this book because Blackness is too often treated as a liability when it is a gift to behold. Creation was birthed out of darkness (and so are we). Our skin, our melanin, is good and God-made. Too many times, we know, our challenges are treated as invisible as we hold up churches, homes, communities, governments, families. Here, like the Clearing in Toni Morrison's novel *Beloved*, we have flesh and soul. We speak our joy and our regret here.

> God doesn't push us to the margins, so I am centering us in this book.

And I want us all to rejoice in the relief of being supported and loved while speaking honestly.

Smallness and silence aren't the story of God for women. In the beginning, the first woman was told to be fruitful and multiply, and she and the first man did this blissfully between Genesis 2 and 3 (note: no childbirth was mentioned). I imagine Adam and

Eve exploring their world, tasting fruits and sniffing blades of grass and flower petals, climbing and swimming to acquaint themselves with the animals that filled the earth, discovering each other and making love. And *that* was good. God didn't build a house for Eve and force her to stay in it. He made Adam and Eve a whole world. And the world, as broken and beautiful as it is, is still ours to steward. Black women have an inheritance of climbing and swimming, tending to animals and discovering the land, finding love and enjoying it.

We are free to talk to the God who created all of this for us. God doesn't push us to the margins, so I am centering us in this book.

Don't be afraid to talk to God. God is listening for your voice.

I pray this blessing over you:

May you feel the presence of God nestle around you as you pray.

As you sit at the table of God's abundance, may you feel God's tender mother-love—a love that does not recoil when you lean in.

Instead, there is a Good Shepherd holding a love that laughs as it carries you.

May your prayer increase your faith in the God who adores you.

May you know that your weakness is as sacred as your strength. When all you have is an ache in the pit of your stomach, or butterflies of joy, may the Spirit empower you to offer those as prayers too. In the name of Jesus, may you abolish good-girl prayers that have you hide from God; may you be fully known by God in all your fear, joy, doubt, shame, silliness, or stillness.

May you lean into the Lord more and into fear less.

May goodness and mercy relentlessly pursue you every day of your life.

And may you know God as your place of rest.

In the name of Jesus, that great Shepherd,

Amen.

Prelude: Speak a Word

Beloved,

what is said,
how it's said,
creates or destroys.

Women talk a lot.

Women
talk
a lot.

Women-talk
a lot.

Statement.
Accusation.
Strength
in/tonation.

Some slander our loquaciousness,
invoke shame.
Sexist? Jealous, maybe.
After all,
everyone's first dialect is called
mother tongue.

Word-connection is born
and cradled between our lips.

Why should we be shamed?
By speaking, we imitate our Father,
an echo of divine creation.[1]
Audacious: we talk to God.
God talks back.
God loves this kind of carrying on.

Women:
talk a lot.

Conversations are sinews of the body of Christ.[2]
By speaking, we weave
together
the space between heaven and earth.[3]
We shrink
the gaps between ourselves and others.[4]
We sing
psalms, hymns, and spiritual songs[5] that strengthen us
        during trying times.
Words and melody cause
Jericho walls[6] of chaos and fear to crumble.

Our songs are God's throne;[7]
we are truth-tellers and chin-lifters.
Our encouragements straighten spines.
We come from traditions of rich oral history,
griots and drums as accurate and epic as books—words are
        our inheritance.
So, talk your talk.
Talk to God, for everything.

God speaks.
By speaking, the Lord formed the heavens and the earth.[8]
John's metaphor for Jesus was
the Word.[9]
At the end of days,
when Jesus ends the madness of sin, the enemies of God,
    and the hubris of man,
the sword He will wield will be
a word.[10]

God still speaks
through His Holy Word and through the wisdom of the
    believing community.
God speaks
in the wisdom of grandmothers and the innocence of
    children.
God speaks
through the Spirit within us.
God speaks
through our gut and intuition.
We communicate with the Lord
through prayer and the counseling ministry of the Holy
    Spirit.[11]
God is fluent in the languages
of our tears, laughter, deep sighs, and groans.[12]

We, as God's daughters, are invited into constant
    conversation.
We are not silenced by God.

What might God create in answer to our spoken prayers?

When We Talk to God About
Our Self-Worth

Good News

Dedicated to Tiffany, who asked about a gospel for Black women

"The Spirit of the Lord is on me,"[1] Jesus said,
declaring the commencement of His ministry.

And the Spirit's activity looked like:
good news[2] for the poor
freedom for prisoners
sight for the blind
freedom for the oppressed
and the year of the Lord's favor.[3]

What is this gospel for Black women?
Dr. Parker said to apply *Sankofa* to your Bible reading—
go back and get what was forgotten.[4]
Oh, we're going back.

Good news means nothing is lost forever;
with Jesus as the Lost and Found.
Everyone the world forgets, Jesus turns back,
picks up, holds close, releases with power.

His disciples forgot the women who
questioned Jesus
cried out to Jesus
got healed by Jesus
anointed Jesus
challenged Jesus
because they weren't as "important."

Jesus turned back and got them
healed their demons
broke their fevers
commissioned them
to run for Jesus
announce Jesus
teach for Jesus.

Some folks neglected us,
named us "Forgotten" and "Inferior"
or, if they wanted to flatter, "Black but comely."[5]
Yet the hereness of us reflects the evidence of God;
we exist despite attempts to erase us.
Our presence indicts hypocrisy.

Jesus is turning back;
He saw us following Him in spite of it all.
What He saw in us looked familiar,
looked like His mama, His friends.
He holds out His nail-scarred, gentle hands to us, says,
"You are My family:
dignity is yours
destiny is yours
a future is yours
redemption is yours
freedom is yours
favor is yours.
Do you believe this?
Good news isn't good unless it's good for *you*."

Says, "We're going back; I'm redeeming your years.
Every door closed to your mother,
I open to you.

Every stifled, secret praise your grandmother uttered,
I unleash in you.
Every town they kept your great-grandmother out of,
I will shake its dust off my feet until they repent.
The thriving of corrupt systems is not a sign of My blessing;
that's just diabolical marketing.
It's not divine consent;
it's just sanctioned violence.
The devil will put up a fight."

But we're going back with Jesus
to see where He sustained our families,
tarried with them.
The Spirit showed them:
a star to follow
water that flowed in the wilderness
refuge in places where death pursued them.
So we know our life is an answered prayer.
So we know the Spirit of God carries us.

We're going back in the gospel story,
wrapping ourselves in the good news
that He loves us
died for us
lives for us
calls us by name
and puts His confidence in us.

And after we go back and get all this,
we're bringing it back with us,
sharing it with the sisters,
lifting hearts and chins with the good news.
Our gospel is the relentless pursuit of us by Jesus, the King;
He wants us in His kingdom and Jesus' love reigns.

Being the Only One

Black Faces in White Spaces

I need Your presence as deep breath after deep breath,
the *ruah*[1] filling my lungs, sustaining me.
Anxiety robs me of the habit of simply breathing;
tension floods every sinew.

Being the Only One feels like ambling through a minefield—
working, performing, existing in my beautiful humanness,
violently interrupted:

Can I touch your hair?
Oh, you went to that school? But, how?
Did you grow up with both your parents, then?
You are so articulate.

Please hold my hand, place Your arm before me as a shield.
Guide me through this minefield.

Tell me:
When should my words drip grace?
When should my words draw blood?
Why do I need to walk through minefields
as they skip through meadows of downy grass,
never questioning their own presence, anywhere, at any time,
never wondering how my being became, to them, exotic?

The wars that created all these mines,
planted like poppies,
intoxicated them to brutal ignorance.

Lord, I am weary.

But peace for the future, for those who come after,
means detonating or defusing mines,
clearing a path for my people
to amble, to breathe deeply, without fear.

Spirit, breathe bravery into my soul.
Counsel me in discernment.
My inheritance is rich with courage and company.
Remind me I am not alone, even if I am the Only One.

Held

For Marielle

I want to know what it is to be held without expectation,
with softness and care, without predation—
a love that thrives in the light and the dark,
unashamed.

You asked me to tell You everything and to pray without
        ceasing.[1]
Well, Father, there's an ache around my shoulders and waist,
longing for touch.

This skin that You lovingly covered me in craves a cocoon
        of care,
an embrace of reverence and not mere lust.

I want to be babied, cradled, adored.
Because You created this tenderness within me, I know it's
        not too much to ask for.

Feeling Myself

I'm feeling myself.

No, really.

My thighs are thicker, my triceps, tauter.
I'm stronger.

I don't let small stuff get to me any longer.

These eyes have seen too much glory;
these ears have held holy stories.

My body is sacred at all times and ages,
from the blush of youth to the wisdom of the sages.

The time God gave me to spend is a gift,
and honey, I intend to use it all.

My neck skin is thinner, my hair, fraught—

I'm older, and though I care about this a lot,

I'm proud. Proud that even now
there's an undiscovered version of me

waiting to come to be.

I'm a Star

A Double Dutch Chant

My mama told me
First impressions last
Don't be too rude
Don't be too fast

But life is funny
Cuz what I see
Is that there's more
Than one way to be me

I've been so slow
I've been so nice
Some took advantage
They didn't think twice

Then I got wise
Found out I'm a star
Try to stop my shine
You won't get far

Like the rising sun
I get brand new
I shine fresh daily
Naw it can't fit you

My glow is custom
Be it faded or bright
Better wear some shades
To take in my light[1]

I may be consistent
But I'm never the same
I consume and grow
My soul is flame

Octavia hinted[2]
At first I found it strange
God's light is growth
And growth is change

Starting Over

My Strongtower,[1]

I need Your refuge. My life has spilled over like a glass jar of marbles: scattered, chaotic. I am tempted to tough my way through this, but I have nothing left. I am out of ideas, out of optimism, and nearly out of hope. When I craft my life through the chaos of my own depleted strength, my story is raggedy. I long to be in the epicenter of Your care, in the stillness of Your sovereignty. I am going to stand there, expectantly, waiting for this page to turn.

I believe You are God of the wilderness.[2] You provide in the desert times. In the midst of parched land, You create springs of living water.[3] When there are no crops or livestock, You send manna from heaven[4]—that is who You are. Hagar named You the God-who-sees.[5]

See me, here, in the middle of starting over.

I trust You to bring provision from unexpected places. I know You will guide me step by step. I believe; help my unbelief![6] Help me to see this new beginning as a fresh start. Where I am afraid, infuse me with courage. When I feel weary, give me a soft place to land. When I must climb mountains of challenge, give me traveling shoes of faith and tenacity. And when I am established and healed, may I boisterously speak of how You kept me every step of the way.

This is an opportunity for newness, and I am going to take it. I trust You to give me the energy and resolve I need when I need it. I am going to stand here in the middle of Your peace and expect You to feed me, shelter me, guide me.[7] I trust the story You are writing for me.

My life is a one-of-a-kind story—make it a page-turner.

Poem for the Queer Child,[1] from Jesus

There are people who use My name
to hate you
to hurt you[2]
to erase you.
How hard it must be for you to even attempt to talk to Me,
how difficult to trust Me.

After every hateful slur,
every time they cornered you in the bathroom or by your
     locker,
after they flirted with you in private and punched you in
     public,
after each spat-out sermon damning you to hell
thrust from lips wet with greed and lust,
logs protruding from their eyes[3] as they stared daggers
     at you.

After all that, here you are,
still—
eyes shining with tears,
longing to be safe in the presence of God
when the company of so many of God's children means
     danger.

People don't need faith when the world already caters
     to them;
they need faith to still feel God even as they feel pain.

You are so brave, my child.
Your faith is a sweet fragrance.[4]

I long for the day when your bravery is no longer needed.
But until that day, dear one, never fear—you can find your rest
in Me.
Beloved, they hated Me too.
I make My home with those whom the world despises and
rejects.
I count your wounds as My own.[5]
I love you.
I love you.
I love you.
Not a love that feels like disgust and distance.
Not a love that says, "Change first."[6]
Not the kind of love that breaks contact and care to
remain holy.

You are my child, and wherever you go,
I am coming after you.[7]
I am with you, always.
My love blankets you, claiming you.
No one can separate Me from you.[8]
In the heavens, we clapped our hands in delight at the
thought of you.[9]
We adore you.
I made you with joy.
My arms are always open to you.

Misogynoir

(hatred of, aversion to, or prejudice against Black women[1])

Intersecting lines of presumption
course through my experience:
hypervisible,
invisible,
diversity hire,
magical Negress,
mammy,
too dependent,
too independent.

Like a tattoo,
these intersecting lines
of discrimination
are drawn upon my skin
by people without nuance
or curiosity.

I am Sara Baartman,[2]
body exploited, gawked at, and dissected
for lurid amusement.

I am Antoinette "Bonnie" Candia-Bailey,[3]
disbelieved by my white supervisor
as I begged for margin
to tend to my mental health.

I am Henrietta Lacks,[4]
dying of cancer,

my body harvested for my DNA,
used for decades
for research and profit
without consent, apology,
or compensation.

I am Serena Williams,[5]
arguing for my life
on my laboring bed
because no one
believes my crises.

I am Sojourner Truth,[6]
reminding people
that Black women
are women.

God of Hagar[7] and Jochebed,[8]

Do You see us used by people who seem so blessed by You? Why do You send us back?

Do You see us loving our children, desperate to protect them, yet having to send them into a world that may be apathetic to their beauty and value? Why not change the world?

Do You not see that to be a Black woman is to be gaslit several ways, not knowing whether people are coming for you because of your race or your gender or both?

Do You see us marching, tearing down racist flags, casting our bodies in front of guns and pepper spray, testifying before hostile panels for the uplift of Black people—but being greeted with silence when we are the victims of injustice?

Do You see all the times our survival is wrapped up in persevering in strength, only to have our brothers complain we're not docile enough?

Have You seen white feminism? There is no freedom there; they want us to be mules for their cause. We are ignored and then accosted by white women's tears when we're not fighting by their side for measures that will benefit only them.

We can't breathe, either.

We need space to discover ourselves out from under the harsh gaze of misogynoir. Where is our space, Lord?

Creator, never do we want to be anything else but Black women: courageous, creative, intelligent, resourceful, community-minded, and mothers to civilization. But it is tiring to fight for the right to exist.

This is what I ask of You: peace. The space to be. And I want Your justice to roll down.[9] Claim me. Show up and show folks that Black women are beloved and worth defending. I want that kind of justice—the kind that abolishes inequity and brings those in the margins to the center. The kind of action that fulfills Galatians 3:28: "There is neither Jew nor Gentile, neither slave nor free, nor is there male and female, for you are all one in Christ Jesus."

I know You want more for Black women.

Make it so. Make it so.

Breaking Glass Ceilings

Architect of Opportunity,

I am here to shatter false boundaries. I will not fear, because You are with me. You created me for this. I trust that You will transform jagged glass into my mosaic of welcome.

The shoulders of ancestors known and unknown, postures straight and strong, have propelled me upward. This is no tower of Babel;[1] I encompass many languages and tribes. I am miraculous.

Do I sound confident? It's because I know You, my Maker, have fashioned me on purpose.[2] I am the culmination of preservation, determination, answered prayers. My life echoes promises made hundreds of years ago. I believe the ransom that You paid for me,[3] through love and through blood, confirms my great worth.

Fear will not rule me today. Fear will not rule me tomorrow. I lay claim to Your promises instead: promises of a hope and a future,[4] of my highest calling,[5] of Your power[6] and wisdom, which You give generously.[7] I will not be intimidated just because I am the first. I am the progeny of survival. I come from a people who have bent foreign tongues to their will, conjured joy from offal and sweat, and learned Your name and Your love despite deception.

"Do not fear" has always been the refrain of your messengers.[8] You're the only one to fear, and You love me. Nothing is left but love and courage now.

I choose to ignore the hecklers. I will not cower to stereotypes. I yield no power to misogynoir.[9] I believe in the support of my community. I believe in receiving help when I need it. I move like a daughter of God, graced with the honor of breaking this glass ceiling.

Maker of Opportunity, sustain me in dignity. Shore up my help. And give me strong arms to reach back and hoist up those who have been blocked by the ceiling I just shattered. And one day, may these shoulders happily bear the weight of future generations.

Job Interview

Jehovah-jireh,[1]

Your Son, Jesus, taught us to pray, saying, "Give us this day our daily bread."[2] I'm asking You about a work opportunity. With this position I can get that bread.

Is this job Your provision, or is it a distraction? Am I pursuing this out of fear and scarcity? Is this job dignifying, or will it diminish and deplete me?

Your Word includes stories of women You have provided for—women who demonstrated courage and tenacity. Ruth moved to a new country and gleaned in the fields for herself and her mother-in-law.[3] Lydia was a seller of purple cloth and showed such strong leadership that Paul founded the church of Philippi with her.[4] Help me to discern between foolishness and faith as I decide on this job opportunity.

Remind me that I interview them as much as they interview me. I bring value, experience, skills, and intangibles that would elevate any workplace. Yet I am holding on to fear about money, poverty, want. Help me to let go of fear in order to take Your hand. You are my Shepherd; I shall not want.[5]

If I don't work, I don't eat, and this reality exhausts me sometimes. Help me to lean not on my own understanding[6] when it comes to income. I want to wisely steward what You have given me and also have faith in Your abundance in my life.

Prompt me to remember that You created me to be more than an income, a title, or a position. My identity as Your Beloved never changes. Your love and care for me keep me every day. Fortify the faith I have in You. Guide me toward the best decision through the wisdom of Your Spirit.

Imposter Syndrome

Great I Am,[1]

I feel like Moses, staring at a burning bush, watching flecks
of flame cover the verdant leaves.[2] I feel the heat but
taste no ash and hear no crackle of burning wood.

I sense You calling me forward.
I am hesitant.

Lord, did Moses think he was hearing things, seeing things
that weren't there?
When You told him that he would lead people into freedom,
did he wonder whether he'd lost his mental bearings?
What? Me? A murderer and a fugitive? An elder with a stutter?[3] *I*
must have eaten some underdone lamb.

You are spurring me forward, yet I doubt myself.
Father, I know ten people with better credentials.
I have talent, but I know others with more.
Where You are leading me, I have seen others go—and fail.
I don't have the experience or expertise that I think I need.

I can't.

Why are You prompting me to do this thing, Yahweh? You
know me!

You know me.

You made me.

You safely cocoon unsinged bushes flanked by flame.
You can ignite a fire that fuels instead of consumes.
You are the God of Pentecost—
Your flame hovered over believers, blazing as a symbol
of Your love, fluent and catching.[4]
You empowered fishermen, tax collectors, and the formerly
        demon-possessed to do the work You had for them—
        ordinary people ignited by Your flame.

Your presence is the empowerment I need.

Remind me that I am no imposter.
You have gifted me to set about this task You've entrusted
        to me.

In a stingy, scarce world, I lack nothing because Your
        generosity goes before me.
I don't need to fear Your flame because You are not trying to
        burn me out but imbue me with Your power.
I can move forward, I can say yes to You, because You are
        trustworthy—and so am I.
I was made to do this.

And when what intimidates me becomes familiar and
        accomplished, I will give You the glory.

For Eve

I didn't know.
I woke up to a world where every answer was "yes" and "let's
    go see."
I didn't know what a river was until I submerged myself in the
    depths.
I didn't know the texture of a lion's mane until I buried my
    face in its fur.
I didn't know I was intoxicated by the scent of my love's neck
until I nuzzled him for the first time,
and then time and time again.
When that glorious creature tantalized me with the offer of
    new knowledge
in this glistening, young world, ripe with discovery,
I took it.

I knew I wasn't supposed to eat that fruit from that tree,
but you have to understand: everything was "yes!" in our new
    world.
The serpent introduced something else I had never
    experienced before: doubt.
It's not that I doubted the Creator as much as I doubted what
    I had heard.
Thought maybe I didn't hear correctly.
Maybe I had misunderstood my love's warning.
If the fruit were dangerous, why would he watch me eat it?
Wouldn't he have stopped me?

I didn't know.
I didn't know betrayal to anticipate it.

I didn't know deception to detect it.
I didn't know death to fear it.

Ignorance doesn't keep us from dying.

God of Eve, Mother of the Living,[1]

Thank You for the example of Eve, the mother of us all. She shows us what it is to be the blueprint without having one.

The first woman to fail and keep going. She existed outside of time, and the land yielded freely, the weather was never harsh, and shame simply was not. She knew no other way to be besides naked. Comfortable in her skin, did she ever feel compelled to hide?

But then the serpent. The fruit. The eye-opening. Then, the hiding. The discipline. What is labor? she must have wondered—and then eviction from the only home, the only state of being, she had ever known.

She didn't know.

That the dizzying changes didn't end Eve is a testament to her tenacity. We women have it too. That she found a way back to love with Adam after his horrible betrayal (he silently accepted the forbidden fruit, then blamed her for eating it, and then had the nerve to name her just like he had named the animals[2]) is the height of her generous forgiveness (and maybe a signal of her loneliness).

She continued to trust You after being cast out. Miraculous.

And You walked with her outside of Eden.

Eve was the first to carry a child and the first to labor to give birth. What did she make of her swelling belly? How did she first know how to feed her Cain? Yet she did; she sustained the lives of those children named and unnamed.

You were Eve's midwife.[3] Eve's story shows us that You can sustain us through the worst changes and the unknown challenges. You are our support in bringing forth life.

Eve was the first to bury a child. The first to agonize over one son killing another over nothing. She was acquainted with the grief of making a man, only to watch him fall. You were there when Adam stood silent. You warned Cain and discipled both Cain and Abel.

We are never alone, even in our crushing grief.

Thank You for honoring Eve's courage to continue after her world changed over and over. She persisted through relocation, redefinition, and even reproduction.

When we see Eve, Father, we can see ourselves: Black women who birth culture, spirituality, style all over the world. Women whose bodies have been vilified and lusted after, gawked at and demeaned—then duplicated. We are the blueprint, but we're often overlooked and underappreciated. Even so, through You, we are indomitable.

We get back up. We persist.

When We Talk to God About Our Bodies

Self-Love Revolution

This was Mary's song after she consented to bear Jesus:

> *He has brought down rulers from their thrones*
> *but has lifted up the humble.*
> *He has filled the hungry with good things*
> *but has sent the rich away empty.*[1]

Mighty One,[2]
You have done great things for me too.
You are healing the places where my ancestors starved and
      scraped to survive; I have provision.
Though those who came before me had to steal away for a
      moment of solace,
I have been blessed with choice and leisure.
You have gifted me with redemption, Mighty One—
empower me to claim it within my own body.
My grandmothers toiled to supplement their meager rations
      by tending their own gardens, savoring the legumes
      and greens they cultivated.
May I savor in peace what my grandmothers fought to grow.

Mighty One,
how can I despise this body?
Loving myself is revolutionary. My body is a marvel.[3] I will not
      abuse it.
But Lord, when I do, forgive and help me.
I have internalized so many lies; I attack myself before
      anyone else does.
I berate the cellulite, the bones.

I demand myself to grow in places and shrink in others.
I criticize the body that has kept me alive.

I am because You are.
You purposely crafted one-of-a-kind me.
My elders say You don't make mistakes; I receive that truth.
My existence is cradled in intentionality.
May I sleep soundly and regularly, cradled in Your peace.
May my relationships reflect my infinite value.
May my nourishment and hydration remind me of Your
        unquenchable love.
May my skin care routine dignify the depth of beauty my
        ancestors bequeathed me.
May I be open to receiving good things from You that put the
        greedy and privileged to shame.

Loving myself is revolutionary.
Your love for me ushers in a new way that topples hatred,
        oppression, and despair.
So let it be.

May my movement and strength training cause my cloud of
        witnesses[4] to clap their hands for joy.
I eat well and grow strong, like Brother Langston said,[5]
        because we were hungry.
But because You have done great things for us, Mighty One,
        we are a blessed generation.

Foundation Matching

In the beginning,
our skin was luminous—
bronzed by a gentle sun,
hydrated by a morning mist,
nourished by the fruit of Eden.

But then, cast out of the garden,
we were introduced
to heat rash and pimples
and quickly oxidizing, mismatched foundation.

White supremacy and greed
resulted in our makeup
as a parody—
blackface coal,
mulatto redbone,
jaundiced high yellow.

But You gifted us with a spectrum of hues,
adorned us
with the creamiest latte
to the most luminous obsidian.

Behold,
You sent forth Your servants—among them:
Rihanna, Pat McGrath, and the OG, Fashion Fair.

Thank You for the trailblazers of makeup for the melanated
because You know that freedom includes the ability to live
       comfortably in our own skin.

Now, I lift to You this moment of gratitude:
my foundation blended like morning dew on a flower's
       delicate petal,
my face and neck perfectly matched,
I can find no flaw in this mirror.

Finally, a foundation worthy of my God-given color.

Alopecia

Glory Maker and Glory Taker,

Are you unmaking me?
I miss my dense, thick hair.
I miss the pillow of it that kept me from sleeping comfortably
      on my back.
I miss my tired arms from twisting twisting twisting after
      taking an hour to wash.
I miss complaining about maintenance, then smiling at my
      results.

I avoid the mirror now.
When I look, I just see empty spaces, like ghost locks,
      lopped off—
snatched.
I took my hairline for granted when it was a strong, dark halo
      framing my face.
Now, I touch my edges and tear up.
I don't recognize myself; I'm staring at a stranger.

I was born with a crown.
You took it from me—didn't You?
Give me back the easy confidence of familiarity,
the routines of all these years, the hair I always had.
I don't want to be unmade.
I wanted to grow old with a white shock of afro or maybe locs,
claiming my elder status through my bright hair radiance.
But I am afraid of aging now. What else will You snatch?

I am stumbling into baldness, stunned.
My confidence, fragile as it was, has abandoned me.
I don't know who I am anymore. I feel ugly.
I wanted to be made better, God, not unmade.
This is not vanity; my hair has been a part of what makes
     me *me*.
It's my glory, isn't it? Where is my glory now? Who am I
     without it?
I am heartbroken. I am clay[1] that You have dashed to the floor.

These shards—what will You do with them?

Cramps

Jesus, be a Midol.

I don't believe periods are a curse, but these cramps are
      about to make me cuss.
Deliver me from this painful heavy-bleeding episode.

Or could You just let these sweatpants stay loose and comfy,
these meds work, this heating pad soothe,
and this ginger ale do its ale-ing?

Scriptures say I can come to You in prayer with anything.
Well, here You go: I am reaching out for the hem of Your
      garment.[1]

Help me, Your daughter.

When the Braids Are Too Tight

Dear Lord, the braids are too tight.
Me and the hair lady 'bout to fight.
Guess I'm stayin' awake tonight.
Pain when I lay down is my plight.
Brows pulled up till I got second sight.
Hope this Tylenol gon' get me right.

On Menstruation

To the One Who Shed Blood and Rose Again,

I always thought You made the period, but You did not like it.[1] All the "unclean" talk confused me; why would You make women this way and deem us unclean for it? The shame You seemed to have about me gutted me. How could I love You with my everything—You didn't love my everything. But Jesus, You dignified every woman You interacted with—every single one. Where society sought to shame and isolate women for their physiology, You approached with the gentleness of a protective brother.

You are not afraid of blood.

When a woman perpetually unclean because her body could not stop bleeding came to You, You let her touch You and receive healing. You called her "daughter." You called her out of hiding and honored her as a cherished relative.[2]

During her next period she must have contended with fear that her disease had returned. Yet each month until her body was done menstruating, she would remember Jesus had healed her. That blood issue, once a sign of disease, now signaled health.

It is an act of worship to respect my cycle—starting with my own attitude about it—and bless You for my monthly fertility status updates. My Redeemer, You also call me "daughter."

You are for me. Period.

May I interpret everything—bodies, laws, the Bible, information, ethics—through the lens of how You reverse curses and transform blood into a sign of life.

New Mom

God of Mary,[1]

I am in awe of what my body has been doing. I have been surviving on four hours of sleep every night for the last several weeks. I can wake from a dead sleep if I hear my baby's whimper.

I can shower and dress and even get my hair looking decent in seven minutes flat.

Lord, what did I do with all the time I had before this little one was born? Time was a currency I spent lavishly—now I pinch seconds like pennies. My efficiency goes up while my energy plummets. I need the kind of Spirit-fueled energy that raised Lazarus.

Everything feels slower now, like I am running in Jell-O. Show me what it means to love and trust You when my world feels so small and yet so relentless. Surely, loving You with my everything can happen while I change the umpteenth diaper. Keep reminding me that acts of worship are faithful actions filled with love that honor You. Mary worshipped when she bore Jesus, carried Him, nursed Him, nurtured Him with every cuddle and coo. She worshipped as she patiently taught Him how to speak, whispered the words of the Law and prophets as His lullabies, held His hands as He learned to walk. Her acts were more holy than if she had gone to the temple twice a day.

Remind me, God of Mary, that I worship when I sing and pray and read the Bible, but I also worship when I am stuck in the house, grubby, for my child's sake, or when I give up dairy, or sleep, to be about Your business of sustaining life. When I resolved myself to the unknown of raising a tiny new human in the face of all that fear and pain and unknowing, I trusted You to deliver me. That is also worship.

You are transforming my knowledge of Your Son through this new life—and through this body, first pregnant and now postpartum. It echoes the nourishing words of Jesus—"Take, eat: this is my body"[2]—with every nursing session, every trip to the bathroom, every time of skin-to-skin. My gratitude for the flesh-and-blood love of Jesus Christ keeps growing.

Like You, may I excel in love. Keep my love nimble so that it never breaks, but can stretch and bend, contract and expand. May my body and its changes, its strength, its vulnerability, and its healing remind me of the custom nature of Your love—as wide as the universe, as delicate as the dimpled fingers of a newborn, as fierce as a storm, as gentle as a lullaby.

Perimenopause

Dear Jesus,

Do You like women?

No, seriously—do You? Because listen: I have dealt faithfully with my period for umpteen years. I waited for this time in life for my period to finally stop, only to discover that a period is nothing compared to rapidly lost estrogen or fluctuating progesterone and testosterone—and I didn't even know I had that much testosterone.

Creator of all our parts—deliver me from atrophy now.

What are these hot flashes and night sweats?

How come I can't remember where I put my keys—I just laid them down!

When did my skin get so dry?

What are these neck wrinkles that weren't here yesterday?

I keep looking back. I am no longer who I was. I have been through changes before—puberty, weight fluctuations, births, surgeries—but nothing like this. I am bewildered and scared. Is this the rest of my life: Gravity pulling me down? Grieving over what used to be?

Women are half the human population, but where's the research on our health after childbearing age? Where are our advocates? Are we lovable and intriguing only between sixteen and forty?

Jesus, out of all the times You talked with women, how many times were those conversations about childbearing? Maybe once—and You steered the conversation from women's bodies to talking about who is blessed.[1] You recognized women as having faith,[2] as sincere worshippers,[3] as people who need healing,[4] and as people who love and take care of You.[5]

The Gospels testify that You desire us to be whole and connected to God. If I take You at Your word, then I must conclude that You do like women.

I pray these truths because I am struggling with how You made us, and I need to be reminded of my worth in this season.

Now I understand why Sarah laughed about having pleasure in her old age.[6] I don't understand why every woman privileged to live long enough will experience the seismic shift of menopause. I need Your help to figure this out. Guide me, Jesus, toward compassionate and knowledgeable medical care. Direct me toward nutrient-dense foods and joyful movement. Curb my tongue before I snap at my people, and keep me free from hot flashes. I need You to have mercy on me, Lord. Have mercy on all of us going through this change.

Yes, Mortal

Thanksgiving for Our Living and Dying Bodies

To the One Who Will Save Me from This Body of Death,[1]

Evidence of mortality abounds in my body. It's a witness of suspicion, strength, scars, and survival. My body is a map of decisions, telling the story when my mind and mouth are too shy to speak. Yes, I carried and birthed children in two different ways. Yes, my skin has been drenched with the mist of Zimbabwe's Mosi-oa-Tunya, the spray of the Pacific Ocean, the Caribbean Sea. No, I don't wear as much sunscreen as I ought. Yes, I have a secret love for toe rings. Yes, oboes and xylophones provoke me to daydream. No, I cannot do squats without my knees cracking.

Yes, I am dying.[2] *Yes, I am living.*

"Pious" men and women ignored my body except to condemn its inherent sinfulness, its ability to tempt men, its refusal to conform to either narrow beauty standards or its narrow calling to bring pleasure and babies. And I confess: I have been just as judgmental of myself—demanding ceaseless work, untenable stress.

Am I frightened? Avoiding the mirror of self-examination? Will I wither if I acknowledge that I am passing away, that I am not powerful? Am I willing to become acquainted with freedom through letting go?

Lord, grant me the knowledge of my mortality and wondrousness.

My Creator, my prayers come through shea butter and cuticle oil as much as utterances and bended knees. I am offering care to this body, this living sacrifice[3] that is yet dying (as all bodies are), while cultivating praise to You for the life I am yet living. Every body is preaching a sermon, and I want mine to preach good news.

May every breaking of bread and enjoyment of wine with loved ones offer gratitude to You because, my Jesus, I am here, creating and loving, receiving and offering strength and a witness because of Your willingness to die for me.

This is my body. Breaking now, whole again one day,[4] by faith, because of You.

That you, my Jesus, kept Your crucifixion scars post-resurrection[5] and then broiled fish for Your friends[6] is not lost on me. Your good news redeems the torn places—nourishes, shares. Your scars bear a testimony: Yes, I died. Yes, I live. You will too.

Lord, may the boundary lines of life keep me in a place of delight and humility, keep my worship sincere, and make my body a witness of God's love.

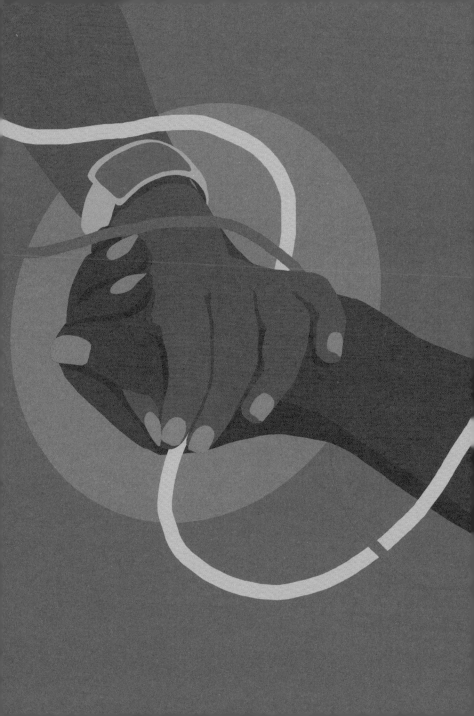

You Can

You are sovereign over mitochondria and cells.
Your eyes don't fail to focus on the infinitesimal.
You can see what we can't.
You can heal what we can't yet conceive.
You can touch a body and cure it.
You mesmerize and dumbfound doctors with a move of
      Your hand.
You confound prognoses with divine improvisations of
      life-giving.
You can make the biopsy results irrelevant—mere evidence
      of what was, not what is.
You can hush damning diagnoses.
So have mercy and do it.
Thank You in advance.

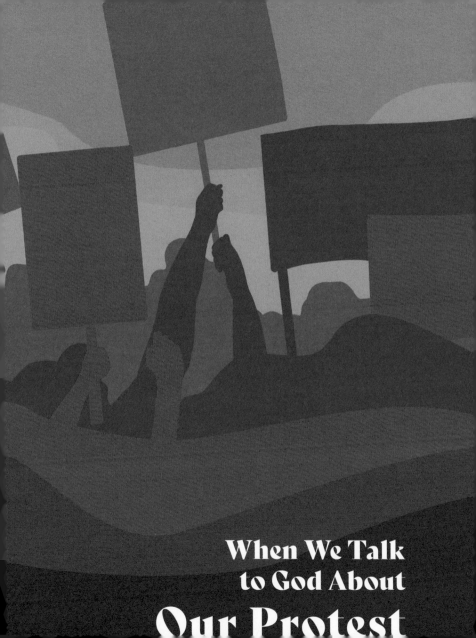

When We Talk to God About Our Protest

Bullies

I wanted to pray for . . .

The bullies who coerce and beat anything into subjection—including the law. Law doesn't even offer a sip of water to parched justice. Justice is an epithet in the mouths of cultists hoping to starve her to death in the name of mammon.

I wanted to pray for . . .

Women who are related to power, content to be the inspiration for destruction, who encourage less education and more baking. Women who call the police to perform violence by proxy; who gossip and blackball behind my back as they smile in my face; who never share, never advocate; who appropriate and steal because comfort dulled their grit and imagination. These who say, "Your children are so clean—will you be my maid?" believing the offer to perennially serve them is the height of generosity.

I wanted to pray for . . .

The people who hate protests but adore insurrections.

I wanted to pray for ...

People so safe and comfortable that they must dream up a future dystopia so that their present violence will appear proactive rather than cowardly. The ones whose jobs, homes, and churches are meticulously planned to exclude people like me, yet expect me to travel past the boundaries of my own safety to amuse them, convince them, help them understand.

I wanted to pray for ...

Those who rail against the marginalized, minoritized, and disenfranchised, yet never pour even a drop of water to justice's parched lips because justice looks like equality, and equality is a threat to the hierarchy they work to maintain.

I wanted to pray for ...

The ways that bullies violate the past for power and profit, concealing history's face to hide her bruises. She just wants to heal.

I wanted to pray ...

But I am too angry.

My Children and the State of Things

Father,

With every birthday, every inch grown, every blossom of their bodies, every follicle of peach fuzz, my children become ripe for state terror. My joy for their birth and their incredible presence in the world is tempered by the fear that they will not be seen as they are, but through the lenses of terrified people armed with state violence.

Father, Your Son grew up in the shadow of empire, spreading healing and truth, but was treated violently. He attracted and fascinated people in the street and the halls of power, drawing both their curiosity and scorn. He was deprived of life by cowards. If Your Son couldn't escape the violence, what hope do my children have?

Help my heart to remember when my nervous system runs feral in fear:

Remember that my children are still here, still whole.

Remember that my inheritance is not a spirit of fear, but Spirit-fueled power, love, and a sound mind.[1]

Remember that my children were created in the mystery of the womb, in the dark, beautiful realm of Your creativity. You made them with such wonder.

Remember that Your Son grew up with a community of extended family, faithful friends, and elders who were generous with their wisdom. In the world of violence that He came to, Jesus still experienced love and care.

Remember that Jesus died but did not stay dead. (I confess: this doesn't comfort me right now.)

I forget that I have hope in Your Son. His sacrifice, death, and resurrection are our hope. I get so scared for my children that I spiral into worry. Help me to remember and trust You.

Would You continue to place good people in the path of my children? People who will speak life into them. People who share their own stories of perseverance, creativity, love, imagination. People who will not let my children languish in self-doubt but will coach them in thriving so they can glimpse You. Thank You for allowing me to witness other people offering wisdom to my children, generously, without finding fault. This is a gift straight from You.

May Your favor shelter my children all the days of their lives.

When They Work Your Last Nerve

Lord Who Commands Angels,

Please, please, please command some mouths to shut before they start talking nonsense—or provide the bail money I will surely need afterward. You said vengeance is Yours[1]—but can I borrow some? No? Okay, so can You assemble Your heavenly avengers and vindicate me?[2] My nerves are working hard to keep me vigilant, attuned, protected, but these folks are working what feels like the last available one. I don't have time for this, God. You, on the other hand, have nothing but time.[3]

Jesus, be a deep, cleansing breath. Can You please treat these trifling people like You did the losers hawking wares in the temple?[4] I am not asking You to turn over money tables (though canceling these student loans would be much appreciated), but just maybe that one person's laptop over there? Can You send Gabriel to hush some mouths like he did to Zechariah?[5] Just give them some time to think and listen, God. A little time just to shut all the way up.

I think You misunderstood me (as if), my good God; I didn't pray for patience or perseverance. You won't catch me asking for virtues I can get only through hardship. I don't want to be tried.

Jesus paid it all, and I would like the dividends of peace, please.

No Justice in the Land

No justice in the land
No peace
Plea bargaining
As justice peeks
Through so-called blindfolds, taking kickbacks
Can't read the law and doomed to break it
Can't catch a break, a chance to make it
In this land of the free
To buy out
Sell out
Or get the hell out
System's evil
Can't represent yourself, we will
For a fee larger than the one you'd pay
Off scot-free at least today

Oh, say can you see
A perversion of justice reigns supreme
Court's a joke
Verdict was written before you spoke
Truth deferred, honesty interred
If you don't have the cash, you get served
The penalties of the guilty ride on the poor
Like playing the coast guard instead of going to war
God's so silent my ears are numb from straining
God bless America, but which god's reigning
The deity of greed, the god of making deals

The one that lines pockets of lawyers who steal
The god of the government
Lying to the masses
Spit in our faces
Kicking our asses
The home of the brave
Is for one who endures
Looks past sickening present
And searches for cures
To society's ills
The salve for the city
Who charges past anger and leaps over pity
To dignity, character, love for mankind
And stands for truth
Even when justice ain't blind

Prayer for the Activist

God of Justice,

We remember Erica Garner,[1] who watched her father, Eric Garner, be choked to death at the hands of a merciless man over loose cigarettes.[2] We heard him gasp, "I can't breathe," desperately whispering his humanity to his murderer. Erica saw this and chose to fight. She fought with a broken heart. Then, she died from a broken heart—too soon, Lord. She didn't even reach twenty-eight years old.

We know the sacredness of justice work. Our heritage is worship through resistance, from Harriet Tubman to Ida B. Wells, from Claudette Colvin to Angela Davis, from EbonyJanice to Tarana Burke. We know You know the fate of prophets and fashion them to have a fire shut up in their bones, burning for righteousness and a better world.

God of Justice, You know that truth-telling can shorten the life expectancy of Your prophets. We pray You would provide protection, that Your love would be a refuge of safety. We pray life over our sister-activist. Keep her heart beating. Keep her eyes clear. Keep her mind sharp. It costs, body and soul, to be an advocate.

But Jesus, You are also an advocate.[3] You said You were a burden-bearer with an easy yoke for the weary and heavy-laden.[4] Lift the weight with her, Lord, so she doesn't collapse. As she remembers the dead, the falsely accused, the wronged ones, the victims, You remember her, oh God. Please—don't leave Your prophet to die. Have mercy. Offer protection. Reward her for her compassion. Bless her with long life and the satisfaction of seeing justice done.

In the 400th Year

In the 400th year,[1]
bound to lend their tears to the mortar,
their bone and nail to the brick,
when the sound of their mother tongue compelled—
scrubbed and raw legislation that bathed
rabid violence into love of country,
baptizing citizens' hands
after they tossed innocents into the mouths of crocodiles,
after they looked through the wailing women
as through the spaces between reeds,

I wonder:
Did the mothers and sisters sing psalms and hymns?
Did the words cotton in their throats?
Did joyful trust gather
like sloughed skin and spit, coating their mouths?
Did they clutch their bellies before they sat in ashes
and think of the ghosts of their wombs?
Did they grieve the birthing stool,
the helpless cycle,
the fruit of their blood and labor turned strange—
split, limp, and soggy?

In the 400th year,
did they go hoarse or numb?
Did they remember the Lord's name?

When prayer became as absurd as birthing baby boys with
    any joy,
how many wailing women bent brick-baking
because their mourning was illegal?
How many sisters watched a tiny hand bob to the river's
    surface—
silently, because survival meant cultivating
a controlled response to massacre?
Murderers can be fragile.

How many did they bury in the sands
as generations slipped into ancestry?
What was freedom?
What good would it do to worship
the One who abandoned them there to be hunted, worked,
    reviled?
What volume could amplify their rage at God's abandonment,
their mother tongue silenced by their oppressors and the Nile
because God stared at the wailing women
as through the spaces between reeds?

How did they love and lay and carry and labor?

What did they say?
What did they do
for God to finally hear?

impossible child

impossible child
they said
her existence an anomaly
every breath borrowed

she vacillates between hubris
(because, baby, existing in spite of is a flex)
and existential angst
(she looks at the night sky and whispers to it,
am I a mistake? or worse,
has God, nestled just out of sight in those stars,
neglected to see me?)

daughter of a barren woman
granddaughter of a woman raped into motherhood
great-granddaughter of a woman who fled

she was birthed into an inheritance
of survival
blood
impossibility
and carbon

no copy, though
but yes, an echo

radicalized from the womb
to be suspicious
of gamblers posing as practitioners
our bodies, their dice, their tokens, their playing cards
theirs: the house that never loses

ours: the weathering
the gaslighting
the neglect
the experimentation
dying
no anesthesia

(bring back the midwives
protecting wombs' constellations
—God said Abram's descendants would be like the stars[1]—
in the face of pharaoh
bring back maternal life)

the impossible child
imagines those tiny bodies floating bloated in the Nile[2]
finds her kinship in limp, dimpled hands
spins the stars backward
through the turning of pages

to Hagar, wilderness sister in the cloud of witnesses[3]
oppressed by a barren woman
raped into motherhood
desperate to flee

does God see
does God see
me

yes
He says
points her back into slavery
to live

her body a witness
her body an indictment

progenitor in the impossible
prone and parched
eyes dimming from the indifferent sun
her gaping mouth and dying son: a question

does God see
does God see
me

God condescends
wears her questions as a name
makes a well
makes them well
a kind of second birth

life?
impossible
yet here she is, just
the same
part
of a constellation of witnesses
impossibilities incarnate
their beingness
their hereness
their heiress
is an act of God

subversive as a manger
under a starry night

A Prayer While Waiting to Vote

We've come a mighty long way.
You've brought us this far, and I won't turn around.
Dogs and horses ran us aground.
Children marched for my future.
Medgar Evers's blood ransomed my ballot.
Fannie Lou Hamer kept going—
sick and tired as she was,
jailed and beaten and stalked.

We are the children of the promise,
the fulfillment of the Dream.
You've brought us this far, and I won't turn around.
I want to hear freedom's sound.
Redistricting won't work,
gerrymandering won't do—
with the memory of my ancestors
and the righteous love of God,
I will come through.

Their resistance won't stop me;
their petty laws are a farce.
This land is my land too;
we stay ready to march.
The long lines aren't new;
the wait times won't defeat me.

My ancestors gave too much
for their pettiness to beat me.
We've come a mighty long way.
I won't turn around now.

My vote is for a better world;
my ballot is a vow.
Democracy is true or false.
The test is what is done
with Black women like me on voting day.
See this republic run
away from life, liberty,
and happiness's pursuit—
when freedom has a darker hue,
they want to make votes moot.
But my presence will indict
the wrong and challenge the offending
until democracy aligns
with the myths that they're telling.

Lord, You've brought us this far,
I won't turn 'round now;
I got the baton, and I'm running this race—
give me strength to keep going somehow.

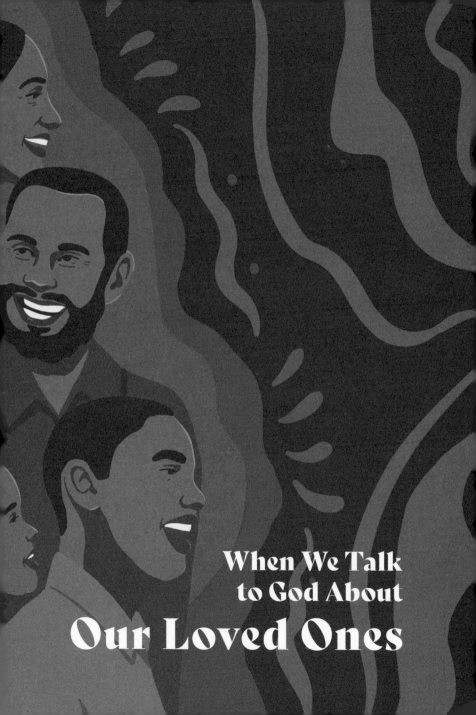

When We Talk
to God About
Our Loved Ones

Prayer for Daughters

You did the absolute most when You created my strong, sharp baby girl (even when she has gray strands and wrinkles, my baby she will always be). My daughter is evidence of Your goodness and creativity.

She has taught me so much about how to spend time with You—I didn't expect that. She is teaching me to stay curious, asking questions when I would have chosen shy silence. She is bold in righteous action, standing up for truth-telling and righting wrongs. Preserve and grow these godly inclinations within her.

Make her attentive to her worth. May her gut be focused on the Spirit's guidance and a trusted resource of inherent wisdom. Keep her heart strong so that she lives through heartbreak. Cause her feet to walk ever in the direction of kindness and integrity. Bless her hands with creativity, tenderness, and the ability to defend herself. Protect her mind from sabotage, both internal and external. Tune her spirit to resonate in the key of Your love. Remind her that every coil, dimple, curve, and color that composes her is good and blessed and holy.

Although conflict and resistance can mature a person, I pray, God, that You would remove nonsense from my daughter's life. No riffraff, no narcissists, no grifters, no leeches, no users.

Proverbs 11:5 says, "The righteousness of the blameless makes their paths straight, but the wicked are brought down by their own wickedness." May the paths of my daughter straighten according to her righteousness and Your mercy, all the days of her life.

Aging Parents

For Joanne

Ancient of Days,[1]

Black does, in fact, crack.

There are tiny fissures, imperceptible at first, obscured to apathetic or careless eyes, but we, the loved ones, see. We are not made of armor but flesh and sinew that can thin and sag, bones that grow brittle. Our minds—repositories of our worries, secrets, brilliance, and wit—can begin to betray us too.

My elders are changing—forgetting yesterday's dinner but sharp in childhood memories. Their taste buds long for sugar and salt, but nothing tastes the same. Limbs slow and shrink. They lie wispy in my arms. I can and do carry them, though I don't feel strong enough, mature enough, ready.

I didn't know I would be parenting my parents. That I would bathe and moisturize their tender skin, ferry them to doctors' appointments, make sure they are eating a balanced diet, make sure they are eating anything at all.

It's an honor and a blessing to care for the people who cared for me, and as far as I am able, I dedicate myself to this privilege. But it still costs.

You knit us from breath, dust[2] and love from the beginning until now. It's no surprise to You, but I still find myself caught off guard. I feel like cartilage, a joint connecting the past and the future, my childhood and adulthood, my children and my parents. I am worn down from the wear, and I need Your strength and patience to love nimbly and keep it together.

Friends

For my friends, but especially my sister-friends

Weaver of memories, Reveler in setting a rollicking table, Harbinger of every good gift, of course You couldn't help Yourself when it came to blessing friendship. You—Father, Son, Holy Spirit—are always supported, loved, in perfect perichoresis.[1]

Remember in the garden of Eden: the one thing You observed that was not good for the first human was being alone. You delivered another human into creation; You didn't even do it the same way because You adore variety. Togetherness was the good and whole vision You intended. Only then was the world You created a place of peace.

Thank You for the togetherness You have given me. Even in this world so far from Eden, I catch glimpses of perfection through my loved ones. I bless You for how You have blessed me. I am wealthy with good friends.

Lord, I have friends who have traveled life's journey with me for so long that they can point out every brave place I have made it through to remind me I can climb to solid ground. I have friends whose voices are a balm to my soul; their mere presence is permission to examine, to rage, to celebrate. I have friends who embody the freedom You have given to me: to make mistakes, to experience forgiveness, to receive loving criticism and to grow from it. My friends have been Your love, Your grace, Your comfort, Your exhortation, and Your joy in my life.

Would You bless them real good, Lord? May favor chase them. May Your love be their canopy and shield. May people be compelled to choose honesty and gentleness around them. May they be clothed with integrity, grit, and unexpected blessings. And may I be found a true friend to them in their times of want and times of need.

Favor for Our Children

Father,

So many of us have been made to feel the cruelty the world can offer a Black child. The presumption that we misbehave more and study less. The surveillance and harsher discipline. The concrete playgrounds, bars on windows, and metal detectors at schools, preparing students more for prison than for university.

When it comes to our children, I walk hand in hand with fear and vigilance. It's not that I don't trust You, my Refuge—it's that I don't trust other people.

Because of this, I can miss the beauty all around us. Please help me to stay vigilant, because I must, but also to recognize tenderness.

Kindness to a child is heaven touching earth. My heart swells in gratitude each time our children are encouraged and loved.

My Present Help, I offer thanks for all the people who have been kind, and who will be kind, to our children. Thank You for the people who see them for the curious, vibrant people they are. Thank You in advance for the people who will be a shield, protecting them from harm, even and especially when their family's not there. Thank You for the many individuals who offer wisdom and pragmatism from which our children can learn. They won't always listen to their mamas—I know because I didn't always listen to mine—but may they pay attention to good counsel.

I pray the path of our children's lives would be lined with favor. May they always be surrounded by people who care for both the color of their skin and the content of their character. Thank You for the people who will cause my children to thrive wholly.

I bless the teachers who have poured hours into instructing our children. So many have managed to teach well and also to inspire our children to rise to academic excellence, to dream bigger, and to imagine a world beyond our present circumstances. Please continue to grace those teachers' lives with provision and otherworldly abundance.

May our children's friends have good sense. Thank You for these future friends with whom our children can be safe, heart and body. When they do dumb stuff, God, cover and protect them and keep them from harming others because they are being unwise.

May danger get lost trying to follow our children. Keep them cloaked in Your safety.

New Grandchild

You have granted me life, my dear Redeemer. In my time, I have walked through valleys, through earthquake circumstances, but You set my feet on a rock, steady.[1] You have been my protection and have preserved the lives of my children. After so many nights of worry, or when I got angry instead of curious, prideful instead of merciful, You still kept me. I grew right along with my children.

Through my love for them, I have come to understand Your love for me. Never in my life could I have anticipated the overwhelming devotion and fierce protection I felt on seeing my grandbaby's face.

This is a love with depths that I simply cannot fathom.

How can I express my gratitude to You, God, Bringer of mercy and sweetness, for the joy You have brought to my life? My heart is so open. Every breath of this child, every wriggle and sigh, is blessing and redemption. I am so grateful for the chance to love and pour into a child again. To correct the mistakes I made before. To love my children through their children. To impart the wisdom I didn't know I had or that I was too harried and busy to see before.

What an opportunity and gift this child is—a reminder to look beyond myself and my generation to fortify and strengthen the ones who come after me.

Father, I want to build a worthy legacy for my grandchild. Please allow me to be a place of peace for this child. I want to be trustworthy and tender toward this child. Grant me the power to heal generational wounds through every cuddle, every conversation, and through the wisdom of both my silences and my speaking.

Bless this child's parents; I know they will need so much grace. I pray to be a source of relief for them in times of sleeplessness or stress. It really does take a village to raise a child, and Lord, I want to be a member of this village. May my grandchild never feel lost or alone as long as I am here to provide refuge.

When the Kids Start Driving

Abba,[1]

I cannot believe my baby is old enough to drive—they're a little less child-like every day. I feel both excited and concerned. Thank You for guiding my baby-who's-not-a-baby into a new stage of life and independence. I am so grateful for the time and freedom I am about to enjoy (when I stop worrying). Liberated from years of chauffeur service. Free from spending hours in school carpool lines, at the mall, sports practice, or music lessons.

My dear Abba, would You grant my children mercy as they leave the house? Your Word says some trust in chariots and horses, but the righteous trust in Your Spirit.[2] It's not the make and model of the car, nor the car insurance (which is too high), that will ultimately provide safety for my child—it's You. I am depending on You, Lord, every time they start the car. Surround them with Your guard and protect them from other motorists—and vice versa.

Spirit, weave sensible habits into their practice so that they look right, then left, then right again; so that they text after they park; so that they drive sober or not at all; so that they know where their registration and proof of insurance are and can easily reach them.

Honestly, I am terrified of potential police interactions my children will have just because they are Black and behind the wheel. God of justice, I pray that You would cause officers to fail if they are violent or scheming. Hide my precious new driver from the clutches of legal bullying.

Bring them back home. I just want them to come back, whole.

Empty Nest

After I restock the fridge
After I deep clean the house
After I bathe and walk around with nothing on—which I
     haven't done in ages
After I play the music I like, loud as I like
After I take the parental controls off my TV
After I watch every show I want, uninterrupted
After I redo my budget and rejoice over more money for
     groceries and self-care—and way less for gas
After I go to bed and wake up in a quiet house
After I consider that each day moving forward will encompass
     this quiet
I will call my child.
I pray You will give them the mercy to pick up when I call
Because they miss me too.
I give thanks for the Next Things that You will grow us
     through
And for the peace of my quiet house.
Give me the energy and perspective to enjoy this season
But also give me the sense of intentional generosity to
     assure my child
That my nest is always here for them, a safe place to land.

Laugh as We Die

Family Secrets Lament

We always smile,
never cry,
laugh as we die.
No one
needs
to know our business.
We sustain
silence
from generation to
       generation.
We say,
"'ow dis pain me so!"
but no one can know.

I'll never forget.

Dad says,
"Never let them see you
       sweat."
Oh, but whispered
history
is a rag soaking this in.

A sixteen-year-old labors
to bear her uncle's child.
Sisters fragmented
reveal shame-stories
       through
poisoned intention
until
all that is heard
are the scrape slide
scrape slide
of forks
on bad china and
rice and peas gliding
gummy
down regretful throats.

I'll never forget.

Dad says,
"Never let them see you
       sweat."

Until
brother's gone mad
sister's gone missing
auntie's obsessed
with which man we're
        kissing
until
Grandmother dies—
didn't know her
        real name.
One girl's not by the
        casket,
the daughter of shame.

That's okay.

We always smile,
never cry,
laugh as we die.
No one
needs
to know our business.

But don't we?
Family?
We sustain
silence.

No one
ever
forgets.

We smile
and we laugh.
We scrape
and we glide
through
birth
through
death
we
worship
our
pride.

After the Argument with Your Husband

Dear God, I asked for this man, [1]

Remind me of the joy softly blanketing the day we made our vows, the tears gathering in his kind eyes as he looked into mine, how his lips were a candy whose taste I became hopelessly addicted to, how I smiled at the scent of him lingering on my clothes—because this man I asked for just disappointed me. Again.

In the book of James, it says You give wisdom generously [2]*—I need Your wisdom so I know the difference between my stubborn pride and my self-worth. With Your wisdom, I can suss out when I am reacting instead of taking in my husband's feedback and presuming his best intentions.*

You also know my husband, Father. He has a little boy in him who needs protecting. Sometimes he thinks he needs to protect that little boy from me. He gets scared. I ask for Your Spirit to intervene, to give us silences in the times we have nothing good to say. To give us words to explain our hurt without cutting each other down. To move us toward resolution and intimacy.

I know my man loves me, and I love him. But when I am triggered, I don't always have the words to describe what I am experiencing. I need You to stand in the gap for us, Lord. You put us together; You want us to stay together—can Your Spirit be our translator during times of conflict? Can You create in me an otherworldly tenderness toward him?

Sometimes I like a good fight—it feels cleansing. But I don't want to stay there, and I know he doesn't want to, either. We want to get back to the loving part. So Father—I am bracing as I ask this—if there is any truth or value to what my husband is saying, help me to receive it. And could You do the same for him, too, please? If it is in my power to bring resolution, give me the humility to bring it about. If I wronged him, give me the strength to apologize without qualification.

We want to break generational curses with our love. We want to hand the next generation a healthier example of marriage. Thank You for reminding me of this goal; help us to stay on task.

I want to travel the road to a healthier marriage with my husband. I trust him. And I trust You.

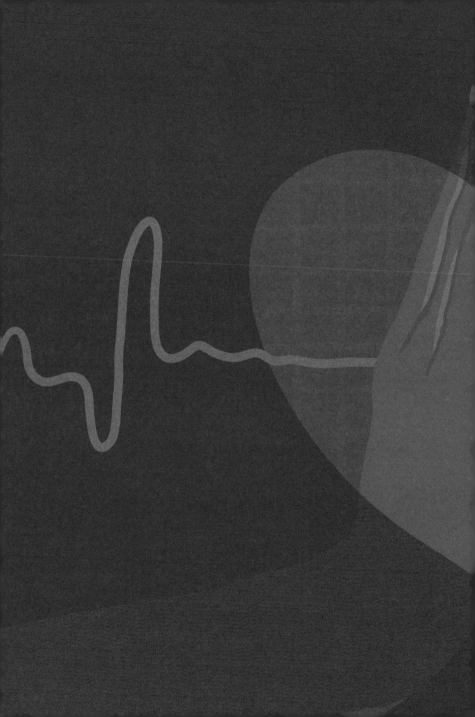

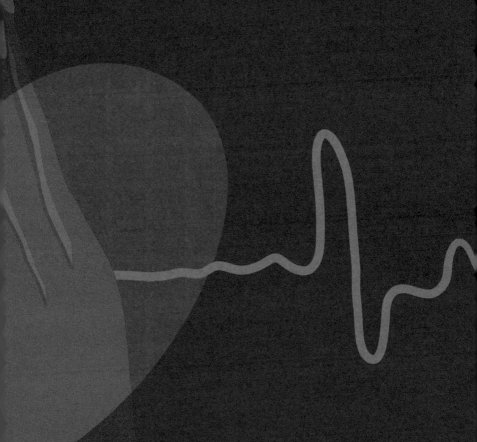

When We Talk
to God About
Our Heartbreak

A Prayer for the End of a Friendship

You are the One who sticks closer than a brother.¹ The One who will not forget me, though my own mother might.² Would You stick close to me now? I feel disposable. My friend—I can't even call her that anymore. I pick up my phone to text her, and my heart aches as I put the phone right back down. Some drama goes down at work, and I hoard every detail, waiting to spill it all while we chat—but we won't have that conversation. I stew over an important decision and naturally want to ask her for advice, but she's not available for that anymore. Not for me.

What do I call her now? She's someone I once knew. Still walking around in the world, still alive, just closed to me.

You are close to the brokenhearted,³ so I know You must be here with me now. I am so grateful that You will always be with me. I just want You close, to help me process all this pain.

What did I do wrong? Was I insensitive? Did I take her for granted? What are the lessons about friendship that I need to learn, Lord? After this pain ebbs away, what wisdom will I have for my other friendships?

I am asking all this to mask the pain. I am devastated. I don't know how to get over the fact that this person who I spent so much time with has decided she doesn't want to be with me anymore. This pain feels worse than a breakup. The rejection stabs deeply. I keep our final conversation on repeat in my mind, attempting to process and to progress, but the ache just stabs me again, and I am pushed back into grief and depression.

She's the person I would call to process my sadness; where do I go now?

I go to You, my good Father. You catch my tears. You mend me. Could You please direct life to go easy on me while I reel from this loss? Can You lift my chin and help me remember that I am not disposable?

Do You think I will ever make a friend again? Will I trust again? I am afraid because I know that if I want a close friend, I will need to be open, vulnerable, and presume the best. But Father, I don't have it in me.

I want to be done missing her. Walk with me through this loss.

Breakup

Kind Cruelty was their name—
the one who took my heart and cradled it before stomping
    out its fire.
Crimson laughter burned through their throat
like the rum of my father's homeland.
I was too intoxicated by its cadences to notice
the needles in their hands.
The dagger words poised to impale me:
"It's not you; it's me."

Just like that, no more lingering kisses,
no more nights wandering the city holding hands.
No more nuzzling into your neck or smelling your scent on my
    clothes.
You made my coffee—a dollop of cream, two sugars.
You always knew when I needed more soy milk.
You used to take my hand every time we entered a room.
You led my grandfather to the good chair to ease his legs.
And you led me to mistake your kindness for love.

Cruel Kindness is Your name—
You, whose grace is surgical; cut, slice, and mend.
My anger boiled at You for all the tears,
those dagger words You let them thrust.
You were supposed to be my heavy quilt in winter,
my cool water in the desert, my present help.
My God, my God, did You forsake me?[1]

You responded with seeming silence when I shouted,
        whispered, cried.

"Why didn't they want me?"

Slowly, my bloodshot eyes cleared.
Your listening ear and Your people were my slow, patient
        revival.
I quit coffee and took up herbal tea
and curled up with good friends and Your Good Book.
Your words smoothed and coated my lonely nerves,
strengthened and sutured my heart.
You bend toward my heart's ear to say,

"I know the plans I have for you."[2]

When Death Comes

Jesus,

How do I pray when I don't have the words? My head, pounding; my eyes, swollen; my heart, broken. God of resurrection, weep with me because my loved one is dead.

Mary and Martha, crying out to You, both said, "If you had been here, my brother would not have died."[1] The grief they felt mingled with disappointment in Jesus' silence—I get that. I know You are here; You just choose to do nothing. Your response feels as silent as the grave. There is no Lazarus moment[2] for me, for them. Just stillness, just cold.

I know You are a man of sorrow acquainted with grief,[3] Jesus. Death is not merely conceptual to You. You were sent violently to Your own death; You felt the ceasing of Your breath,[4] the stopping of Your heart. You know what it is to die.

You know what it is to mourn. I am sure You mourned Your earthly father Joseph's death. We didn't get to read what that was like for You. Maybe You didn't have the words, either.

You wanted to withdraw and process the death of Your cousin, John the Baptist. You didn't get a chance before the people's needs and disciples' ambitions pulled You away. You hardly touched Your own grief before healing others.[5]

But You didn't raise John the Baptist back to life—Your own cousin. You loved him, You honored him, but You did not raise him again.

I sit with that now, in this stillness of mourning. I wonder how the Spirit can stand not breaking through the distance between heaven and earth to raise every dead thing. It must be counter to the Spirit's nature to leave things without breath.

Lord, I never wanted to see my loved one like this. It's an image I will never forget. I feel the weight of holding on to the witness, the last memory of them being here, but it's a heavy burden to remember.

I know You are good, but death? Death is not good. People have tried to comfort me by saying this is Your plan and my loved one was ordained to die. But didn't You come to conquer death?[6] I am ready for death to die.[7] I am ready for the day to come when death stops winning.

Oh God, this ache is consuming me. But this ache is all I have left of my beloved. I just want them back. I just want to hear their voice one more time. I want to hold them and have my love for them flow to them because I don't have the words.

I don't know how I am going to make it through the next hour, day, week. Will You carry me? I can't stand up under this alone.

When You Bury Your Parent

I need You to help me keep living. Before I knew Your name to call upon, I called theirs.

I don't remember the first days they sustained my tiny new life. They must have been exhausted. As I grew, they did too, learning the art of discipline, negotiation, mentoring, parenting. They didn't get it right all the time. But looking back, I see how they sloughed off so much trauma to parent me into more wholeness than they received. They protected me in ways they weren't protected.

The days and nights I had to wash dishes, thaw the meat, clean the bathroom, and look after my siblings, my parents took shifts, tired but determined to keep a roof over our heads and food in our bellies. They said without words that I was worth sacrificing for.

I tried them. I broke rules and tested boundaries. I voiced my resentment loudly. I know I hurt them. Their love, steady, was my lighthouse. My port in the storms of life. Deep down I knew that even when I acted a fool, I could take my prodigal behind right back to their loving arms.

Where do I go now? I feel lost. Orphaned. I want to lay in that coffin too.

I can't stop the ringing in my head, the constant loop of remembering that my parent is gone. I'll never hear their voice again. I'll never wrap my arms around them again.

Oh God, this is too much to bear. I've never lived without them in the world. How do I keep going? I can't function. I'm numb. I'm devastated. I keep forgetting to shower. I lie awake, desperate to sleep, but when I sleep, I don't want to wake up. When I wake up, I remember all over again: they are gone and they are not coming back. I remember their body, lifeless and still. Light, gone. I don't want to remember.

I know their aching and troubles are over. I know they reside in peace with You, but I want them with me. I wish they didn't—we didn't—need to endure death to find that peace by Your side. Jesus wept when He witnessed death[1] and agonized as He experienced it,[2] so I refuse to call death "good." I hate death with every fiber of my being. I believe You hate it too.

I need You to help me keep living. Without my parent here, I'm in between not wanting to die and not knowing how to take up the mantle of life. I need room to grieve, and I need to feed myself. I don't know how to engage with life while I'm buried in grief.

Movin' On Up

A Psalm 121 Remix

I am down here
where the earth cracks, too hot and tired,
where you can't get caught slipping,
where money is protected, but people? Disposable.
I am looking up; I want to see You.
Maybe if we lock eyes,
You will come down and change things here.
I know You haven't fallen asleep on the job, right?
You stay woke.
Can You move me up a little higher?
I want to look at Your face,
higher up. Your face shines.
I know who You are:
Maker of the air I breathe and the land I tread upon . . . Maker
        of me, of us.
I know what You have done: You've kept me.
Nights we would have starved, You fed us.
You have delivered us into days we thought we wouldn't live
        to see.
Here, where the politics are dirty, and the guns, plentiful.
Here, where love is fickle, and therapy, unattainable.
Here, Your watchful love will be a covering of supernatural
        safety.
Lift us, move us up to a safe harbor.
Expand Your loving attentiveness over me and over us
today, tomorrow, and for life.

Miscarriage

Oh God, My God,

I knew.

I knew the baby was here, but now the baby is not here. It's hard to explain to other people that I am walking around with a hole in me, that I am hollowed out and grieving.

Father, to explain the hole, I have to explain that I was pregnant. I am not ready for the past tense. My baby was a miracle whom I carried. I imagined my child's features—bright eyes and chubby cheeks—and I pictured the day I would hold my baby in my arms. My arms ache with emptiness now.

Help me. I don't know whether to speak or just not talk about it, but I don't want to pretend just to make other people comfortable.

I know, Lord, that other people look at me and see a whole person because they don't look closely enough at my red-rimmed eyes and dry hair and the way I touch my belly absentmindedly. I am hollowed out, not whole.

Lord, I feel like a walking sepulchre. A living tomb. Brown, sticky truth seeps onto my panties. I want to bleed out. If I pass out, I can't think any more about hope's blood between my thighs, lifeless. About why I cannot expand this family. About how I feel like a hostile place for life.

Hope was a faint pink line.
None today. Just blood and no line. No hope.
I feel empty.

Empty.

After an Abortion

Can I talk to You about this?
After what I did, are You still my God?
Have I forfeited the right to ask You for help?
Will You hear my prayer?

This prayer is my act of faith.

I couldn't see this pregnancy through—it hurts to
    confess this.
I know how valuable life is to You, how precious.
Life is precious to me, too, if You can believe that.
Can You?

You allowed Your Son to die, to save many.
You know of loss, of difficult decisions of life and death.
You know.

I am not trying to be blasphemous.
I want to reach out—do You understand?
Do You understand—I had so few choices.
I couldn't see support in my future, not even from You.
No angelic visit for me.
No last-minute miracle money.
No village to raise this child with me.
No reciprocity or equal weight of responsibility.
The woman is required to carry life, and her entire being
    contorts to accommodate the change. It's elective for
    the man, like taking French or gym class.
I couldn't do it. I couldn't see it through.

My body couldn't. My family couldn't. My finances couldn't.
I feel relief and grief. And a lot of anger.
I long to live in a world where I could mother this child.
Where I could provide for them and surround them with love.
Where I could know that we'd both have heat in the winter
        and the light bill would always be paid, and we would
        never know struggle, food insecurity, stuckness.

I chose myself. I had to. But I feel the loss.
I stare at babies in strollers.
I wonder how much they would weigh in my arms, the scent
        of their skin after a bath.
I am not a monster.

Are they with You?
Are they whole now, smiling and giggling at the sight of You?
Do they know that I miss them, even as I wrestle between
        resolution and doubt about the choice I made?
And You, do You still love me?

I read that nothing can separate us from Your love[1]—does that
        apply to me?
Can You receive the questions of Your daughter?
I recognize the audacity of this prayer,
but You are God, You hold all things together, and there is no
        lack within You.
You don't struggle, You don't know fear,
and yet—You will never be a woman in my position.
Do You understand how complex this is?
The hole in my heart and my womb and the harshness of this
        world that asks too much and offers too little?
I still need You. Please draw close to me.

Not Knowing Our Mother Tongue

God of Pentecost,[1]

Sometimes my tongue feels heavy and swollen and dry because its muscle memory has dementia. It is parched for a language lost somewhere.

The Atlantic.

The whip.

Somewhere gone, this language woven in my DNA but frayed at the edges of times past.

I know the end, for it is written: ten thousand tongues sing, nations and tribes intact and distinct, each face—a glory—singing to the Lamb.[2]

God of origins, why does a whiff of mountain mint bring tears to my eyes? Why do blues and greens and the Indian Ocean bring me peace? Why do the shape and shade and smiling eyes of some feel like home?

I long for the unwritten part: resolution. The question marks on my soul finally smoothed into sighs of understanding. When You introduce me to the plan of us and show me all the torn strands—You love a genealogy moment, don't You?—then I, too, can recite in full my version of "the God of Abraham, Isaac, and Jacob."[3]

You are the God of my great-grandmother, my grandma, my mama, me. We are enough, but we are not all.

Oh, to see the tribes and nations that formed us, remembered in our cadences, our music, our coping ways, our birthing ways, our burying ways; to press my soles into the soil of redeemed, remembered land—unfathomable foundness.

I long for the unwritten part: revelation. When, as in the book of Isaiah, Your holy coal singes my mouth[4]—not because I am a woman of unclean lips, but because You desire my complete praise from a loosed tongue, because Your Spirit inspires utterances unfettered by colonialism, because this language lost to me is a prodigal longing to come home.

And then, I will sing! I will sing to You in every language I know and should have known. I will sing the rhythms of my grandfathers, the meter of my grandmothers, the range of laughing children. I will sing, and the chasm formed by empire will be a distant memory; for every valley of grief will be pulled up and every mountain of trauma will be leveled. Freedom and wholeness will be my song, and my praise will reflect the shalom[5] of You.

A song echoes in my blood. Unburied. A hum for now, until I know the words. Pulls me up and around and plays like a playground chant when the world is white noise. Moans a canopy of love over me when the world is burning. I know it's there because I am here.

There is a song with words I don't yet know. I'll sing the lyrics of this life to You in the meantime, until it's time.

Tourniquets[1]

Don't silence me
as if my words are a redundancy,
a useless appendage on an otherwise sleek body.
I am a member,
God said so.[2]
You might not recognize me,
but I was created to be here.
Cut the tourniquets
from my neck, my tongue,
and you'll see color return.

You'll recognize the sound
of this lamentation.
It's ancient.

"Black lives matter"
is just a remix of
"Let my people go."[3]

Offensive phrases to pharaohs, already free,
chants of freedom to those who languish in chains.
Moses took a knee in Pharaoh's court,
exhorting to end the oppression.
Pharaoh just wanted to see him turn staffs into snakes.
Pharaoh needed pyramids more than Jews' lives to matter.

Same song here:
after ripping bodies from home, land, language, dignity,
the masters of Manifest Destiny

ripped the pages of Exodus from the Bible,[4]
censoring God Himself.
This is America's inheritance.
We have Black churches today because white churches built
        a wall in the 1700s.
The most fortified American border is a color line
made of bricks from our own blood, hair, and bones as
        America calls for more walls.
"Segregate and dehumanize" should not be the policy of a
        Christian nation,
yet here we are four hundred years after the *White Lion*.[5]

I know nothing will change
because comfort is too sensuous an idol.
So many have been indoctrinated to tighten the tourniquet
        on my tongue,
to segregate and dehumanize my words along with my body.
Many of my siblings in Christ refuse even to see me,
much less protect me.

I fight for a dream deferred, and it makes my heart sick.[6]
Yet I still cry out.
My God, You see us here, hurting.
You make ways out of no way.
Let Your people go!
Create a way out of no way for this blood-sodden land.
Remove the stones from hardened hearts.[7]

Let *all* your people go:
the children dehumanized and
the children beguiled by the kingdoms of this world.

Are you God-with-us[8] as we are murdered and abused and
        cast off?

Are you God-with-us when we are called
lazy welfare queens woke DEI CRT criminal animals thugs
        illegals
instead of bearers of Your image?

I need You to speak:
"Let there be life!"
Resurrection—
make all things new,[9]
starting with Your mangled Body.

My people find a kinship in Your suffering.[10]
You said, "This is My body, broken for you,"[11]
yet some siblings waste Your sacrifice,
finger paint with Your blood,
cram Your limbs into bricks to build the very wall You
        abolished.[12]

Jesus, turn Your blood into the wine of gladness.
Turn Your body into the bread of life.
Exorcise the demons.
Make the unclean spirits of this age flee in terror.
Fill Your Body with the Holy Spirit;
a fire in our bones.[13]
And please—remove these tourniquets.
Let your wonder-working blood flow freely,
nourishing us all.

Not colonized or assimilated—
contrite repaired repaid reconciled holy washed clean
altogether human
all together
celebrating Your image in us and in other people
free to worship—every one of us—free.

When We Talk to God About Our Joy

New Home

My Refuge,

Thank You for this space, a physical reminder of Your protective care over me. This home is more than a sturdy roof and a warm, dry place to retreat to during stormy weather. What makes a home is the presence of love, a sense of security, a sacred place where Your peace dwells.

I acknowledge that I live on land that was stolen. You hate the movement of boundary lines in order to steal land.[1] I want to acknowledge the first peoples who lived on this land and pray that they are reunited with it. May Your jubilee[2] come through. May Your boundary lines be marked with justice and flourishing, from sea to shining sea. No one is free until everyone is free.

You are welcome here. May Your presence always be comfortable in this home. Whether I pay rent or a mortgage, the land is not my possession but a sliver of Your world that I get to steward, and I pray I steward it wisely, with Your direction.

Spirit of God, I welcome You to fill this home with good counsel, wisdom, discernment. May I be quick to be still and listen to You as I wash dishes, take out the trash, sprawl on my couch, curl up to read. I don't have to wait for Sunday service to be in Your presence because my home is also Your sanctuary.

May Your Spirit move beyond these walls to bless my neighbors. May they flourish.

Give me the fortitude and joy to love my neighbors as myself. Thank You for opportunities to be a safe place where they are protected and seen.

I pray this house would be a sanctuary of safety and no harm would occur here. I pray You would cleanse this space with Your presence and sweep away any histories of harsh words or horror stories that may have dwelt here before. Redeem it, Lord.

In Your movement to make the earth as righteous as it is in heaven, start with me, here, now.

The Perfect Bite

Creator of Taste Buds,

Sweet, savory, toothsome, smooth, luscious, crunchy. Aromas from Grandma's kitchen on Thanksgiving Day or the scent of grilled burgers wafting on the summer breeze. (Listen, even the unctuous umami of kale satisfies me. A miracle!) Oh, how food can be holy. When I read in the Old Testament Your guidelines for acceptable sacrifice, I knew You loved a good cookout.[1]

I want to tell You: You did exceedingly, abundantly above all I could ask or think[2] with the glory on this fork today. Something about the way this hits compels me to give You praise. The blessed assembly sings a chorus of "she put her foot in it!" Indeed, she did. And she is me. Jesus, I see why You named Yourself the Bread of Life[3] and asked us to remember You with a meal.[4] You didn't want us just to talk about You; Your life has texture and aroma and offers daily, life-giving nourishment. You want to inhabit our lives as we remember You through our bodies as well as our souls—and I remember You now. You could have given us only what we needed for nutrition, but You gifted us abundance through beauty, variety, and taste, preaching through our senses, "Taste and see that the Lord is good!"[5] This perfect bite is a reminder that You provide not only what I need to survive, but also what I crave so that I can enjoy this life. For this, I give thanks.

The Phone Dropped but Didn't Break

For all the times it has tumbled from my pocket or purse,
for all the times I tripped on the charging cord,
for all the times I handed it to my child, whose hand slipped,
for all the cases I've run through,
for all the times I balanced it on the corner of the counter,
only to forget and bounce it off with my hip,
for every time I held it with my shoulder and then got tired
        and looked up,
for every time my toddler used it as a hammer,

Lord, You knew.
You knew my budget.
You knew my limits
and performed miracles.

My phone may have cracked, but it did not break.
I may have to jiggle it a lil bit, but it's still here.
I rejoice in the small things You do to keep me.
I have been bumped, bruised, and misused.
But like this silly little phone,
You've kept me.
Dear God, I am still here.

Good Hair Day

To the One Who Crowns Us All,

We offer praise for the crowns God has placed on us, sisters.

Our hair is stunning. Honestly, every day is a good hair day. Favor ain't fair.

Our hair can resist gravity or work with it.

Our hair can be close-cropped or flow below our waists. We can dye it, braid it, weave it.

Our hair reflects Your creativity.

Our hair protects us from the sun and defies the rain.

Who but You could have made our tresses so well suited to the world?

We're made in Your image, and You are resplendent. Today, with this good hair day, we shine too.

We give thanks for that baldie that accents cheekbones and shows off a perfect head.

We give thanks for the coils that defy gravity and humidity and frame your face like a bouquet.

We give thanks for the regal locs that reveal your distinctly
Black beauty.

We give thanks for the sprouts of hair that came back after
the chemo; they survive and reemerge, just like you.

We give thanks for your relaxed tresses, bouncy and sleek.

We give thanks for that silk press—we see that shine!

When You crowned us, Great Creator, You gave us so much to
work with. You didn't have to, but You did. Thank You.

Delicious Brunch

F(l)avor Bringer,

Rest sneaks in sure and surprising in the rise of buttermilk pancakes or the way champagne bubbles tickle my nose. The swirl of cream languidly flowing, mingling in my coffee, rising, rising.

It's how the repose beams in on a ray of midday sunshine, warming my skin, communicating that I am alive, present and full and giggly.

But most of all, the rest slips through in sonic stealth, through the belly laughs of loved ones. The mm-hmms of affirmation when I tell them about that person annoying me at work, or that one who hasn't texted me back, or that cutie over there kinda staring at me while we're brunching. Each mm-hmm a customized mix of audio affirmation, legions of meaning in each variety: "So what happened next?" "Oh, sis, you are too lovely to wait on that ole raggedy text." "Ooh, I see that look! They fine too."

Thank You for this refuge, Abba, this time when the only demands are rest, fullness, and connection. You set aside a day of rest because You knew we'd need it; we are made to take breaks and slow down. You know that what makes these brunches so delicious are not just the bennies and mimosas, but the relief found in leisure time with friends, the release of tension from my neck and shoulders, and the required deep breaths that precede laughter or tears.

I see this as the sacred space it is—the table You have prepared for me. I raise my glass to You, my Provider, in gratitude.

When It's Your Song

Swing, sway
eyes closed
to feel everything
This rhythm soaks through my pores
so potent the melody
I can see into the past
Before she let go[1]

Mama's giggling as she grabs the kitchen towel
Let it absorb the dishwater
while she absorbs the music
swing, sway
eyes closed

The music, a thread of joy—
unspeakable, full of glory[2]
our full humanity in hush hollers and juke joints
drum circles and choruses
we lift every voice and sing[3]
the songs sewn into us
even through dementia,
immigration,
Middle Passage

Every little thing is gonna be alright[4]
because the precious Lord
takes my hand[5]
and dances me through a melody cloud of witnesses
who wove life into the music

who snatched the thread of joy
and sewed family and persistence and swagger—
loud and raucous
much more important than the dishes

Worship is the hymns and prayers and faith, yes
but I see You, my Good Shepherd,
when this song comes on, and I am reminded
of my mother's smile,
when I use the ears You gave me to revel
and this body You made to respond

Worship is appreciation—
then sings my soul, my Savior[6]
You are so great
I am singing songs in the key
of the life[7] You gave me
I am not alone as I
swing, sway
eyes open as You dance me toward the finish line[8]
In this song I am lost and found[9]

A Marriage Blessing

To the One Who Joins Us Together,

Is there a recipe for a flourishing marriage?

Our relationship ingredients vary daily. Some days our seasoning tastes like our ancestors guided us, and the meal is a feast. Other days, there's only wilted spinach and rancid milk in the fridge, and our wallets deny us takeout.

Lord, would You grant us the willingness to flex and improvise in our marriage? We believe that through the power of Your Spirit, we can persevere through conflict, challenge, and change together. We can respond—together—with humility and mutual trust.

On our wedding day, we said yes in advance to supporting each other through an unknown future. We had no idea what was in front of us, how we'd change, what our convictions would grow to be—still, we both said, "I do."

That takes faith.

Jesus, when You observed a large, hungry crowd coming toward You for help and healing, You asked Your disciples how to feed them: "Where are we to buy bread so that these people may eat?" Philip freaked out, saying: "Impossible! Ain't enough money or bread for us to feed all these people, Jesus!"

Yet You told everyone to sit down, a boy volunteered some sardines and rolls, and You blessed the food and fed the crowd. They ate so well that they were full before the food ran out.

You perform miracles that rise out of hunger and impossibility. Before the boy with sardines, before the blessed bread, You already knew what You would do.[2] When You ask a question, Jesus, You already know the answer. Like the miracle of the hungry crowd, the miracle of a flourishing marriage grows when hunger and impossibility meet You.

In our marriage, You want to guide us toward togetherness and maturity. Growth that we cannot manufacture or buy. Growth that comes only from the practice of faith.

When we find ourselves without the ingredients or skills for a challenge we face, Jesus, will You whip up something for us? Will You take our resources, even our lack, and create a way out of no way? Keep us joined together? We trust that You will feed us in a way that we just can't do for ourselves.

You already know what You are going to do in and through our marriage. You got us.

We want to thank You, our loving God, for the blessing of being cared for by a community excited to support us. Some of these folks will have the bread and fish that You will use to bless us. It might look like wisdom for how to fight fair, how to mourn a miscarriage, or how to practice our faith as a couple.

Give us wisdom to discern nourishing advice; words that don't come from a place of competition or pettiness, don't violate our boundaries, and answer a question we've been asking.

Lord, even if we don't have one perfect recipe for a flourishing marriage, we're good. We have the people, the loaves, the fish, and You, the Divine Chef—who has surrounded us with everything we need.

Arriving

God, I wonder at Your detail in creating me.
Crafted to sense, to experience, to inhabit beauty and
      deliciousness,
You, Divine Maker, formed my anatomy for joy:
naked and unashamed.
You even sculpted a spot just for pleasure.
(Maybe to balance out the childbirth and periods? I don't
      know why You did it, but I am grateful.)
This body gives thanks.
You crafted me for thrill and passion, tension and release—
not merely for work, or excretion, or reproduction.
What does this say about You?
You are a generous and creative God who takes joy in our rest.
What does this say about me? I am made for many things,
and one purpose is to enjoy the body that You gave me.
I aim to reconcile myself to myself, wholly, because You made
      me, body and soul, both.
Every good and perfect gift comes from You.[1]
When I experience this full-body joy,
I will not feel shame before You,
the One who made me capable of this . . . arrival.
I thank You.

A Prayer for Creatives

Living Water,[1]

Life is an opportunity to create.

You created me as a spring, not a pond. Never stagnant, I flow. Living water streams through me, sourced from the heavens. I cannot lack, because You are my source. Creativity is always available to me. I may be momentarily blocked, but it won't last. That block could be my heavenly cue to rest, dream, or snack. Blocks are pauses; they do not define me. A pause is my green pasture, not my doom, because I have the promise of an easy yoke and rest from You.[2]

The prophet Isaiah said that I will mount up on wings of eagles and run like youths,[3] and I can have energy that I need, when I need it.

It's not over for me.

If I try to count myself out because of my age or stage, remind me that the prophet Joel said Yahweh can restore the years the locusts have eaten.[4] Time is nothing to a timeless God.

Creation is sacred work, but it's heavy. My burden-bearer, Jesus, will hold and tend to my emotions as I work. The Spirit will hover over me and inspire me. I am not alone.

The Lord is near. I will feel the weightlessness of God's help. God will bring people who can help me with the burden too. I dismiss the need for independence and lean into the collective care I need in order to create. I will ask for help.

God wants my flourishing. God gifted me on purpose. I cannot fail. The witness of the book of Jonah confirms that God will bring me back to Nineveh's work,[5] even if I try to slink off to Tarshish to escape His call—and that is grace. I cannot miss my chance to do what God has ordained me to do. Even if I do the "wrong" thing, I have a Shepherd who guides me back on the paths of righteousness for His name's sake.[6]

I am loved, held, and guided by the living God.

Travel Mercies

Waymaker,

When You formed the world from Your words, created the depths of the sea and populated it to thrive in the dark; when You spoke the galaxies into the far reaches of space and time; when You kissed mountain ranges with snow, You knew. You knew that humanity would cultivate daring and curiosity: the need to witness, journey, and press on to the unknown. You have been the catalyst for movement from the times of Cain (whom You marked so he would not be murdered, wherever he wandered[1]) to Abraham (whom you called to leave his country, and from whom You made a nation[2]). Jesus sojourned from the heights of heaven to the depths of the earth, and back again, to dwell among us and make a way for us to return to You.

Because of all this, travel can be sacred. Though it may be a quick jaunt to the grocery store or dropping off children, we still need Your mercy to get to our destination. We need You as we run errands, and we need You as we cross the globe. In any great travel epic, there are opportunities along the way. As You show us mercy, protecting us during our sojourn, would You cultivate sensitivity to the world around us? Would You compel us to slow down enough to observe the worth and beauty You've given each person in our path? We will travel with expectancy, anticipating the divine appointments You will make for us along the way.

When We Talk
to God About
Our Faith

The First Day

Yeshua[1] began His human days swaddled in the darkness of
      Mary's womb:
birthed into the night air,
heralded by a constellation of the heavenly host,[2]
an echo of Creation's genesis.

When God made the evening and the morning
the first day,[3]
God made the night go first:
swaddled the fresh world in velvet luminosity,
shushed and brooded over by the Spirit.

And yet we struggle against the night,
reject her call to rest,
obscure the wonder of stars with artificial light;
no longer blanketed in hushed wonder,
we colonize the dark spaces all while pondering
the genesis of our restlessness and dragging.

There's a better way.

Let the twinkling stars be our night-light,
blanketing ourselves in the velvet of dark rest;
let our day begin with night's mothering.

Shh—there, there. Cease striving.
Lay burdens down on the pillow of twilight.
Listen to cicada songs.
Bathe in moonlight.
Let the evening begin the day.

"Good" Friday

The word *good* twisted into a crown of thorns,
violence inverted into love,
crucifixion inverted into kindness,
defeating death by dying.
A sinless man condemned, scourged, and murdered—
Good, we say.
I lament that "Good Friday" feels like a polite version of
     "Crucify Him,"
a calm and congenial call for Jesus' death.
To call it *good* means, in the most genteel way, that we need
     Jesus dead too,
that a dead Jesus is good . . . for us.
We call a day of crucifixion
a day of scourging, screaming, bleeding
a day of lynching the most beautiful being in all of existence
a day where the God-man cried out and breathed His last
Good
Friday.

It's a theology of Sunday to call Friday *good*—
a jump ahead to resurrection, even as the blood spills and
     the skies darken.

I lament that we cannot sit with the horror of Friday without
     equivocation,
that we commodify the cruelty of Jesus' death
rather than grapple with our benign acceptance of it.
We fill our homes and adorn our bodies with crosses,
not in memoriam, but as trophy.

We are too comfortable, desensitized, to Jesus' death;
we've normalized His murder,
replayed it on repeat with casual indifference.
Like George Floyd with a knee on his neck;[1]
see it enough times and our eyes grow accustomed.

Emotionally calloused as a hangman,
we shrug off the snuffing out of innocents;
we string fresh-cut flowers around the crucifixion
like a funeral wreath, masking the stench,
lest we inhale death and smell our own numbered days,
sense our own dank sin.

We tie the word *good* like a garland around this murderous
    Friday
to pretty up the grisly cost of sin.

Good Friday wasn't good for Jesus;
crucifixion was a cup He wanted to pass on.
His brow bore that crown both in agony and in love.
We focus on the love and turn Jesus into a mirror;
we look to Him only to admire ourselves, all clean.

I Don't Want to Talk to You

Lord Over John the Baptist and Job,

It's not that I don't know the power of prayer; it's that I do. I know You are real, close, and capable of the miraculous.

I know.

But right now I feel like miracles are for white girls with money. Miracles are like heavenly lottery tickets; anyone can play, most of us won't win.

Yet here I am, waiting for the miracle of Your presence and action, stubbornly believing You will answer me. Even as I talk to You, I wonder: What's the point? You are God. You already know I haven't showered in days, and I send my friends' calls straight to voicemail. I cry so much, I carry toilet paper rolls instead of tissue boxes. How do You see me like this yet do nothing? You know what I have been through. You know every scab of every cut from every time I've trusted You and got wounded by Your stillness. Is Your inaction intentional? You can move, but You don't. You can speak, but You choose silence.

I don't like how this feels—especially when evil is out here prospering. Some truly wicked people—people who don't fear You at all—continue to scheme, steal, and bully their way into thriving. They sure look blessed from where I stand. I am broken and waiting for You to bless me like You bless them.

You said You wouldn't leave or forsake me.[1] Where are You? I need You. Where are You?

I don't think I can weather another trial.

I don't want a testimony of survival; I want to be sheltered and soft and inexperienced with hardship.

Why won't You move?

I have heard my grandmother pray. Watched her slowly descend to her knees, humble before You. Heard her plaintive voice call You by Your names: Healer, Provider, Present Help, Banner, Lord of Hosts, Savior. I don't have the grace or piety of my grandmother. I don't have her wide-spread, sheltering tree of faith—all I have is this raggedy seed of mustard.

Your Word says I don't need more than a tiny seed to move mountains.[2] I don't want to move mountains; I want to move You. I want Your ear inclined to me. I don't want the theory of You or the study of You; I want You to show up like a good father. Protect me. Comfort me.

Deliver me—not in some abstract, super-spiritual way, either. I don't want to talk to myself anymore. I want the evidence of Your presence. I don't want Your love to feel like neglect. I believe You when You say that You are light and love; I want to shine from the clarity and warmth of Your love. No shadows. Give me the glow that Moses got.[3] The still, small voice that Elijah heard in the wind.[4] Speak my name, like You did with Mary Magdalene[5] when she knew it was You who called her.

I don't want to be strong; I want to be rescued.

I don't want to persevere; I want to be delivered.

Patience

God Above Time,

One more time. One more breath. One more week. Ground me, please. I want the blossom of fulfillment, but first comes the cracking open of the seed. The death that precedes the germination of promise. The sprouting of new possibilities, nourished by Your superintending care, and the people and circumstances that cultivate the dream. Fulfillment takes time, but I wait impatiently.

I don't want to wait. I keep looking toward the future fulfillment. I am missing the present love, care, opportunity, and provision You have given me. As I wait, I desire to be grateful. Slow my pace enough to see the beauty that surrounds me: the breath in my lungs, the friends who check on me, the song that moves me. I see my privilege; I can luxuriate in anticipation because my now is peaceful. I am fed. I am warm. I have access to clean water. The urgency of survival is not my portion. I want to thank You for the shelter and abundance that I too often take for granted. The choices I make are the dreams of my ancestors, fulfilled.

Who You are in the waiting is who You are in the fulfillment. You are trustworthy, long-suffering, merciful, and full of loving-kindness. You are the manna in the wilderness before the promised land. You are the protector of covenants; You keep Your promises—from the time of Abraham to my time, right now. When You say yes, no one can dare say no.

The plans You have for me are better than any I could concoct if I had my own way. My growth and strength will be fortified by the patience I learn to lean into.

Your plans for me are worth the wait. I will trust You.

Inspection

I was told that God wears white gloves
swipes His finger
finding the corners
of hard-to-reach
shame

checks for dirt
behind the rib cage

requires spit-polished souls
zero tolerance for mess

I wanted to pass inspection

I made my spirit an incurious loft
spare
quiet
each nervous, curated choice
a vacuum
static-free
beyond challenge
so pristine
so stainless
there were no fingerprints
as if no one
lived there

Jesus walked in
did not wipe His feet

dirt and ash
clung to Him

I was afraid
white-glove inspection
and all this dirt

He laughed
clapped his hands
in streaming rays of sun
particles of dust
glistened
hung
cradled in light
that laid bare every speck
I missed

He smelled intoxicating
fresh earth and charcoal
tragedy and resurrection

live
He said

there is dirt
there is dust
there is light

Beloved,
I don't wear white gloves

When You Can't Pray

Hang on.

Today was once the future.
Last year, ten years ago—
times now known but once unfathomable to you.

Do you remember what hurt you then?
Do you remember how you got through?

Remember.
Remember the heartbreak that healed.
Remember the money that covered the cost.
Remember all those colds and flus, how your body carried
        you, how you healed.
Remember the precious tears you once cried, a torrent of
        sadness.
Remember that they dried up, with time.
Remember the sound of your laughter.
Remember the breeze and the gentle sun on your skin.
Remember scratching the itch and sighing with satisfaction.
Remember singing so loud, dancing to your song, letting it
        seep in like good medicine.
Remember your heart; put your hand over your chest, close
        your eyes, and feel how it beats, still.

It's been beating since you were in the womb.
You've grown accustomed to being a miracle—
and sister, a miracle is exactly who you are.

The symphony of circumstances that created you and kept
        you is composed by the Divine.

Sometimes the present notes of disappointment and
        sadness
are revealed to be melodies of protection and progress,
keeping you from further harm.
That job didn't end you.
That relationship didn't end you.
The sickness didn't end you.
The death of that loved one didn't end you.

You are still here.
Please choose to stay here.
Remember and cherish that you are still here.
If that's all you can do right now, that is enough.

I'll pray for you:

Jesus, I bring my sister before You now.

You are a man of sorrows, acquainted with grief.

I know her depression won't scare You.

You don't turn away from our honesty or our pain.

We don't need to clean it up for You.

Would You break through in my sister's circumstances?

Would You pull her from the pit of despair and surround her with opportunities to breathe, to rest, to heal, to experience support and peace?

I pray Your mercy over her.

You are the one who sees and lifts up women.

Your life was surrounded with women who You trusted with Your life. You are safe. You care. You see and hear.

Intervene, Jesus.

Break through in a way that my sister can witness,

so specifically that she knows it is Your work, Your love.

Notes

Introduction

1. Matthew 6:9–13, KJV (spacing and punctuation mine).
2. In Judges 11, a warrior named Jephthah made this vow to the Lord: "If you give the Ammonites into my hands, whatever comes out of the door of my house to meet me when I return in triumph from the Ammonites will be the LORD's, and I will sacrifice it as a burnt offering" (vv. 30–31). His daughter came out to greet him, and rather than turn back on his vow, he sacrificed her.
3. Judges 19 is one of the most disturbing chapters in all of the Bible. It demonstrates how far the Levite (who should have been God's priestly representative) and those who followed him had strayed from God. First, he had a concubine, which is suspect. Then, when men of the city he was visiting threatened him with rape, he gave them his concubine instead. They abused her and left her for dead. The Levite felt offended, so he cut her up into twelve pieces and sent each piece to a tribe of Israel. This is depraved. She received no tenderness, help, or protection from her people or from the people of the city.
4. Genesis 38.
5. Joshua 2:1; 6:25; Hebrews 11:31; James 2:25.
6. Joshua 2:9–13.
7. The book of Ruth.
8. 2 Samuel 11.
9. Richard Whitaker et al., eds., *The Abridged Brown-Driver-Briggs Hebrew-English Lexicon of the Old Testament: from A Hebrew and English Lexicon of the Old Testament* (Houghton Mifflin, 1906), 649.1. "2. נָכְרִיָּה foreign woman, as term. techn., in Pr, for harlot (perh. because harlots were orig. chiefly foreigners)."
10. Julia Jacobs, "Anita Hill's Testimony and other Key Moments from the Clarence Thomas Hearings," *New York Times*, September 20, 2018, https://www.nytimes.com/2018/09/20/us/politics/anita-hill-testimony-clarence-thomas.html.
11. Don Lemon Tonight, "Combined Videos Show Fatal Castile Shooting," CNN, CNN.com, accessed August 1, 2024, https://www.cnn.com/videos/us/2017/06/22/philando-castile-facebook-and-dashcam-full-mashup-video-ctn.cnn. (CONTENT WARNING: this video contains violence.)

12. "Malcolm X: 'The Most Disrespected Person in America, Is the Black Woman,' Speech to Women—1964," Speakola, accessed October 6, 2024, https://speakola.com/political/malcolm-x-speech-to-black-women-1962.
13. Matthew 23:37.
14. Luke 15:8–10.
15. Isaiah 42:14; 49:15.
16. James Swanson, *Dictionary of Biblical Languages with Semantic Domains: Hebrew (Old Testament)* (Logos Research Systems, Inc., 1997). "רוּחַ (rûaḥ): n.fem.; ≡ Str 7307; TWOT 2131a—1. LN 12.1–12.42 Spirit, i.e., the divine Power of God."
J. A. McGuire-Moushon, "Divine Beings," in *Lexham Theological Wordbook*, eds. D. Mangum et al. (Lexham Press, 2014). "πνεῦμα (pneuma). n. neut. spirit, breath, wind. Usually refers to the Holy Spirit, the spirits of humans, or immaterial beings; occasionally refers to breath or wind."
17. Romans 8:26.

Prelude: Speak a Word

1. Genesis 1:3.
2. Ephesians 4:29.
3. Matthew 6:10.
4. Ephesians 2:19.
5. Colossians 3:16.
6. Joshua 6:20.
7. Psalm 22:3 KJV.
8. Genesis 1:1–3.
9. John 1:1.
10. Revelation 19:21.
11. John 16:13–14.
12. Romans 8:26.

Good News

1. Luke 4:18.
2. James Swanson, *Dictionary of Biblical Languages with Semantic Domains: Greek (New Testament)* (Logos Research Systems, Inc., 1997). *Gospel* (or *euangelion* in Greek) means "good news": "εὐαγγέλιον (euangelion), ου (ou), τό (to): n.neu.; ≡ DBLHebr 1415; Str 2098; TDNT 2.721—LN 33.217 the

good news, gospel (Mt 4:23; Mk 1:1; Ac 15:7; 20:24; Ro 1:16; 2:16; 10:16; 1Co 15:1; 2Co 4:3; Gal 1:6; Eph 1:13; 3:6; 6:19; Php 1:27; 1Th 1:5; 1Ti 1:11; 2Ti 2:8; Rev 14:6; Mk 16:15 v.r.)."

3. Luke 4:18-19.
4. In the context of her New Testament scholarship, Dr. Angela Parker said, "To reclaim my Womanist identity after moments of gaslighting, I often have to take 'Sankofa' moments and 'go back' psychologically into the past to read beyond assimilation and color blindness." A. N. Parker, *If God Still Breathes, Why Can't I?: Black Lives Matter and Biblical Authority* (Eerdmans, 2021), 55.
5. This is a reference to an awful but popular translation choice made in Song of Songs 1:5.

Being the Only One

1. J. A. McGuire-Moushon, "Divine Beings,' in *Lexham Theological Wordbook*, eds. D. Mangum et al. (Lexham Press, 2014). *Ruah* is the Hebrew word for breath, wind, or spirit. "רוּחַ (rûaḥ). n. fem. breath, wind, spirit. Can refer to immaterial beings as well as to wind, breath, human spirits, and the spirit of God."

Held

1. I Thessalonians 5:17 KJV.

I'm a Star

1. Matthew 5:14-16.
2. Octavia Butler, *Parable of the Sower* (Headliner Publishing, 1993). Butler wrote "God is change" to succinctly define the new religion Lauren Olamina (main character) formed in her dystopian novel.

Starting Over

1. Proverbs 18:10.
2. Exodus 16:9-18.
3. Exodus 17:1-7; John 4:13-14.
4. Exodus 16:11-12.
5. Genesis 16:13.
6. Mark 9:24.
7. Psalm 37.

Poem for the Queer Child, from Jesus

1. This child may be your inner child, who has longed for love for a long time. This child may be the person you parent, or teach, or your sibling. In any case, may the love of Jesus wash over you, beloved.
2. Matthew 5:46 is about loving people with whom we disagree.
3. Matthew 7:3–5 NASB.
4. John 12:3; 2 Corinthians 2:14–16.
5. Isaiah 53:3–6.
6. Romans 5:8.
7. John 3:16–17.
8. Romans 8:39.
9. Zephaniah 3:17.

Misogynoir

1. *Merriam-Webster Dictionary*, "misogynoir," accessed September 3, 2024, https://www.merriam-webster.com/dictionary/misogynoir.
2. "Sara 'Saartjie' Baartman," South African History Online, August 16, 2013, https://www.sahistory.org.za/people/sara-saartjie-baartman.
3. Leah Asmelash, "An HBCU Administrator's Suicide Is Raising Painful Questions About Black Mental Health," CNN, February 27, 2024, https://www.cnn.com/2024/02/27/us/hbcu-lincoln-university-missouri -suicide-questions-black-mental-health/index.html.
4. "The Legacy of Henrietta Lacks," Johns Hopkins Medicine, accessed October 6, 2024, https://www.hopkinsmedicine.org/henrietta-lacks.
5. Maiysha Kai, "Serena Williams Pens Essay on Her Near-Fatal Birthing Story," TheGrio, April 7, 2022, https://thegrio.com/2022/04/07/serena -williams-essay-near-fatal-birthing-story/.
6. "Compare the Two Speeches," The Sojourner Truth Project, accessed October 6, 2024, https://www.thesojournertruthproject.com/compare -the-speeches.
7. Genesis 16, but especially verse 9.
8. Exodus 2:1–10.
9. Amos 5:24.

Breaking Glass Ceilings

1. Genesis 11:1.
2. Psalm 139:13.
3. Mark 10:45.
4. Jeremiah 29:11.

5. Philippians 3:14.

6. 2 Timothy 1:7.

7. James 1:5.

8. Genesis 15:1; 21:17; Exodus 14:13; Deuteronomy 3:22; Joshua 1:9; 1 Samuel 12:20–21; 2 Chronicles 20:15; Isaiah 44:1–5; Jeremiah 1:8; Daniel 10:19; Matthew 10:28; 28:5, 10; Luke 1:30; 12:32; John 14:27; Acts 18:9; Revelation 2:10 are just *some* of the passages containing this phrase.

9. *Merriam-Webster Dictionary*, "misogynoir," accessed September 3, 2024, https://www.merriam-webster.com/dictionary/misogynoir. Misogynoir, n., "hatred of, aversion to, or prejudice against Black women."

Job Interview

1. James Strong, *The New Strong's Concise Dictionary of the Words in the Greek Testament and The Hebrew Bible*, Vol. 2 (Logos Research Systems, Inc., 2009), 47. "יְהֹוָה יִרְאֶה Yehôvâh yireh, yeh-ho-vaw′ yir-eh′; from 3068 and 7200; Jehovah will see (to it); Jehovah-Jireh, a symbolical name for Mt. Moriah:—Jehovah-jireh."

2. Matthew 6:11 KJV.

3. Ruth 2:2–3.

4. Acts 16:13–15, 40.

5. Psalm 23:1 KJV.

6. Proverbs 3:5.

Imposter Syndrome

1. Francis Brown et al., *Enhanced Brown-Driver-Briggs Hebrew and English Lexicon* (Clarendon Press, 1977), 217–218. Exodus 3:14; John 8:58. In Hebrew, "I Am" is transliterated as "Yahweh" (an earlier transliteration is "Jehovah")—a name so holy that it is typically called "The Name" and not uttered in the Jewish faith. "יְהֹוָה n.pr.dei Yahweh, the proper name of the God of Israel—(1. MT 6518 יְהֹוִה (Qr אֲדֹנָי), or 305 יֱהֹוִה (Qr אֱלֹהִים), in the combinations יהוה אדני & אדני יהוה (vid. אֲדֹנָי), and with prep. בַּיהֹוָה, לַיהֹוָה, מֵיהֹוָה (Qr בַּאדֹנָי, לַאדֹנָי, מֵאדֹנָי), do not give the original form. 𝕲 and other Vrss follow the Qr. On the basis of Ex 20:7; Lv 24:11 יהוה was regarded as a nomen ineffabile (vid. Philo de Vita Mosis iii, 519, 529), called by the Jews הַשֵּׁם and by the Samaritans שׁימא. The pronunciation Jehovah was unknown until 1520, when it was introduced by Galatinus; but it was contested by Le Mercier, J. Drusius, and L. Capellus, as against grammatical and historical propriety (cf. Bö 88)."

2. Exodus 3:2.

3. Exodus 3:11; 4:10, 13.

4. Acts 2:1–4: "When the day of Pentecost came, they were all together in one place. Suddenly a sound like the blowing of a violent wind came from heaven and filled the whole house where they were sitting. They saw what seemed to be tongues of fire that separated and came to rest on each of them. All of them were filled with the Holy Spirit and began to speak in other tongues as the Spirit enabled them."

For Eve

1. Genesis 3:20.

2. Genesis 2:19–20.

3. Genesis 4:1.

Self-Love Revolution

1. Luke 1:52–53.

2. Luke 1:49.

3. Psalm 139:14.

4. This is a reference to Hebrews 12:1, which calls back to the people of faith in Hebrews 11. These faith-filled people were ordinary except for their great belief in God, despite their circumstances.

5. Langston Hughes, "I, Too," Poetry Foundation, accessed October 6, 2024, https://www.poetryfoundation.org/poems/47558/i-too.

Alopecia

1. Isaiah 64:8.

Cramps

1. Matthew 9:20–21 KJV.

On Menstruation

1. Menstrual law can be found in Leviticus 15:19–33. In Leviticus, lots of everyday goings-on are considered "unclean"—sex and nocturnal emissions are two other examples. Everybody was unclean at different times. I wonder whether these unclean times were not reasons for ridicule, but instead, time-outs from God—times when people could recover and rest.

2. Matthew 9:20–22: "Just then a woman who had been subject to bleeding for twelve years came up behind him and touched the edge

of his cloak. She said to herself, 'If I only touch his cloak, I will
be healed.' Jesus turned and saw her. 'Take heart, daughter,' he said,
'your faith has healed you.' And the woman was healed at
that moment."

New Mom

1. Luke 1:26–28.
2. Mark 14:22 KJV.

Perimenopause

1. Luke 11:27-28.
2. Matthew 15:22-28.
3. John 4.
4. Luke 13:10-17.
5. John 12:1-3.
6. Genesis 18:12.

Yes, Mortal

1. Romans 7:24.
2. Isaiah 40:6-7.
3. Romans 12:1.
4. Romans 8:11.
5. John 20:27.
6. John 21:7-13.

My Children and the State of Things

1. 2 Timothy 1:7 KJV.

When They Work Your Last Nerve

1. Romans 12:17-19 KJV.
2. Psalm 35:24.
3. Psalm 90:4.
4. Matthew 21:12.
5. Luke 1:19–20.

Prayer for the Activist

1. Vivian Wang, "Erica Garner, Activist and Daughter of Eric Garner, Dies
   at 27," *New York Times*, December 30, 2017, https://www.nytimes.com
   /2017/12/30/nyregion/erica-garner-dead.html.

2. Andy Newman, "The Death of Eric Garner, and the Events That Followed," *New York Times*, December 3, 2014, https://www.nytimes.com/interactive/2014/12/04/nyregion/04garner-timeline.html#/#time356_10551.
3. 1 John 2:1.
4. Matthew 11:28–30 KJV.

In the 400th Year

1. In this piece, I am observing the parallels of the 400-plus years of the Israelites' time in Egypt, including their harsh enslavement, and the 400-plus years of the oppression of Black people in the United States.

impossible child

1. Genesis 22:17.
2. Exodus 1:9–10, 22.
3. The "cloud of witnesses" refers to Hebrews 12:1, which talks about the people of faith outlined in Hebrews 11. These people include Abraham and Sarah, who enslaved, sexually exploited, and abused Hagar (Genesis 16, 21).

Aging Parents

1. Daniel 7:9.
2. Genesis 2:7.

Friends

1. *Merriam-Webster Dictionary*, "perichoresis," accessed October 9, 2024, https://www.merriam-webster.com/dictionary/perichoresis. *Perichoresis* is a theological term created about 1500 years ago to describe the essence of Godness through which the Trinity relates. It is a term that strives to define divine interdependence and love. I adore this word because I adore what it stands for.

New Grandchild

1. Psalm 40:2.

When the Kids Start Driving

1. Romans 8:14–16.
2. Psalm 20:7.

After the Argument with Your Husband

1. If he is *not* a good man, you need to pray and also act, sis—right away. If your safety is compromised, if your children are in jeopardy, if that man is cheating or verbally or physically or financially abusing you, you need to pray for discernment on whom to talk to who will help you up and out of your current situation. You need to flee.
2. James 1:5.

A Prayer for the End of a Friendship

1. Proverbs 18:24.
2. Isaiah 49:15.
3. Psalm 34:18.

Breakup

1. Psalm 22:1.
2. Jeremiah 29:11.

When Death Comes

1. John 11:21, 32.
2. John 11:43-44.
3. Isaiah 53:3.
4. Mark 15:37.
5. Matthew 14:13-14.
6. 1 Corinthians 15:54-57.
7. Revelation 20:14.

When You Bury Your Parent

1. John 11:35.
2. Matthew 26:38-39, 27:45-50.

After an Abortion

1. Romans 8:39.

Not Knowing Our Mother Tongue

1. Pentecost was originally a Jewish harvest festival. God chose this symbolic day to begin a different harvest—that of people who would trust in God—as described in Acts 2. The Spirit descended on the

Jewish believers in Jerusalem (who had recently watched Jesus ascend into heaven) during the harvest celebration that brought Jewish people from all over the known world. The Spirit granted these Jewish believers the ability to understand and speak different languages.

2. Revelation 7:9.
3. Exodus 3:6, for example.
4. Isaiah 6:5–8.
5. James Swanson, *Dictionary of Biblical Language with Semantic Domains: Hebrew (Old Testament)* (Logos Research Systems, Inc., 1997), electronic edition. Hebrew for "peace," wholeness. שָׁלוֹם (šā·lôm): n.masc.; ≡ Str 3073, 7965; TWOT 2401a—1. LN 22.42–22.47 **peace, prosperity**, i.e., an intact state of favorable circumstance (1Sa 1:17); 2. LN 59.23–59.34 **completeness**, i.e., the state of a totality of a collection (Jer 13:19); 3. LN 21.9–21.13 **safeness, salvation**, i.e., a state of being free from danger (Ge 28:21); 4. LN 23.129–23.141 **health**, i.e., a state of lack of disease and a wholeness or well-being (Ps 38:4[EB 3]); 5. LN 25.80–25.84 **satisfaction, contentment**, i.e., the state of having one's basic needs or more being met and so being content (Ex 18:23); 6. LN 34.1–34.21 **friend, companion**, i.e., one who has an association with another with affection or regard (Jer 20:10); 7. LN 88.66–88.74 **blessing**, i.e., the content of the act of giving kindness to another (Jer 16:5); 8. LN 12.1–12.42 unit: יהוה שָׁלוֹם (yhwh) **Yahweh is Peace**, i.e., the name of an altar (Jdg 6:24); 9. LN 12.1–12.42 unit: שַׂר שָׁלוֹם (śǎr šā·lôm) **Prince of Peace**, i.e., the name of messiah (Isa 9:5[EB 6]).

Tourniquets

1. *Cambridge Dictionary*, "tourniquet," accessed October 6, 2024, https://dictionary.cambridge.org/dictionary/english/tourniquet. "A tourniquet is a strip of cloth that is tied tightly around an injured arm or leg to stop it bleeding."
2. 1 Corinthians 12:12–14.
3. Exodus 5:1; 7:16, 8:1, 8:20, 9:1, 9:13, and 10:3.
4. Michel Martin, "Slave Bible from the 1800s Omitted Key Passages That Could Incite Rebellion," NPR, December 9, 2018, https://www.npr.org/2018/12/09/674995075/slave-bible-from-the-1800s-omitted-key-passages-that-could-incite-rebellion.
5. "First Enslaved Africans Arrive in Jamestown, Setting the Stage for Slavery in North America," History, August 13, 2019, https://www.history.com/this-day-in-history/first-african-slave-ship-arrives-jamestown-colony.

6. Proverbs 13:12; Langston Hughes, "Harlem," Poetry Foundation, accessed October 6, 2024, https://www.poetryfoundation.org/poems/46548/harlem.
7. Ezekiel 36:26.
8. Matthew 1:23.
9. Revelation 21:5.
10. Philippians 3:10.
11. 1 Corinthians 11:24 KJV.
12. Ephesians 2:14.
13. Jeremiah 20:9.

New Home

1. Deuteronomy 27:17.
2. Leviticus 25 talks about the time of Jubilee every forty-nine years. Every seven years was counted as a Sabbath year for the people and land to rest and rely on the Lord's provision. Jubilee was the seventh consecutive Sabbath year—a divine reset and restoration season, when debts were forgiven, enslaved Israelites were liberated (no freedom for foreigners, which is wack), and ancestral lands were returned to their rightful owners. Happily, Jesus shows us that God's freedom and generosity is for everyone.

The Perfect Bite

1. You can see this in the first chapter of Leviticus.
2. Ephesians 3:20 KJV.
3. John 6:48.
4. Luke 22:17–19.
5. Psalm 34:8.

When It's Your Song

1. Maze, "Before I Let Go," *Live in New Orleans*, Capitol Records, 1981.
2. 1 Peter 1:8.
3. James Weldon Johnson, "Lift Every Voice and Sing," Poetry Foundation, accessed October 6, 2024, https://www.poetryfoundation.org/poems/46549/lift-every-voice-and-sing. "Lift Every Voice and Sing" is also referred to as the Black National Anthem.
4. Lyric borrowed from Bob Marley and the Wailers, "Three Little Birds," *Exodus*, Island Records, 1977.
5. Thomas Andrew Dorsey, "Precious Lord Take My Hand," Unichappell Music, 1938. This hymn was one of my grandma's favorite songs.

6. "How Great Thou Art," written by Carl Boberg in 1885 and translated by Stuart Hine in 1949.
7. This is an allusion to the unparalleled album of Stevie Wonder's, *Songs in the Key of Life*, (Tamla Records, 1976).
8. A remix of Hebrews 12:1–2.
9. This is an allusion to the lyrics in verse 1 of "Amazing Grace," written by John Newton.

A Marriage Blessing
1. John 6:5 NASB.
2. John 6:6.

Arriving
1. James 1:17.

A Prayer for Creatives
1. John 4:10.
2. Matthew 11:30.
3. Isaiah 40:31.
4. Joel 2:25.
5. Jonah tried to run in Jonah 1:1–3, but a storm and some reflection time within a big fish brought him around to reluctant obedience by Jonah 3:1–3.
6. Psalm 23:3.

Travel Mercies
1. Genesis 4:13–16.
2. Genesis 12:1–3.

The First Day
1. Rick Brannan, *Lexham Analytical Lexicon to the Greek New Testament* (Lexham Press, "Ἰησοῦς" 2011).
   Yeshua is the Hebrew, non-Anglicized version of "Jesus." Greek transcribers attempted to transliterate His name from Hebrew/Aramaic to Greek, which is from where "Jesus" is derived.
2. Luke 2:13–14.
3. Genesis 1:5.

"Good" Friday

1. "How George Floyd Died, and What Happened Next," New York Times, nytimes.com, May 25, 2020, https://www.nytimes.com/article/george-floyd.html.

I Don't Want to Talk to You

1. Hebrews 13:5 KJV, loosely quoting Deuteronomy 31:6, 8.
2. Matthew 17:20.
3. Exodus 34:29.
4. I Kings 19:12.
5. John 20:16..

Acknowledgments

I write this with tears—happy ones. I am one of God's children, and I feel the weight of privilege in being granted the opportunity to write a book encouraging honest connection with God. Lord, Your generosity and loving-kindness is overwhelming. I hope that You are pleased. Green pastures and still waters, You are.

To you, the reader: I am so grateful for you. Your time and mental space is of such value—thank you for picking up this book. I pray that it encourages you. I just want you to know that you are loved and cherished by God. I am cheering for you.

Nothing I have done has been done in isolation. I realize I come from community; and any words I use, I was taught. So many Black women have tutored me in love, boldness, honesty, and devotion to God. I already know this list is inadequate.

I wish I could thank my Grandma Vinola, who bequeathed me a legacy of tactile spirituality, and whom I miss terribly. Some people know the Bible, but my grandmother knows Jesus.

Thank you, Mommy. Every bit of love you have, you give. You are generous. You have persevered. Thank you for showing me what devotion to God looks like. Thank you for never once sowing seeds of doubt within me—you are a bouquet of "you can do it!"

My aunts Georgia, Mae, and Shirley, for mothering me, keeping my confidences, plying me with rice and peas and fried plantain, and taking me on excursions to experience the breadth of the world, unafraid (as long as you were holding my hand with that Jamaican vise-grip)—thank you.

Thank you to Joanne and Rhea. You are my shea butter, slumber party shenanigans, peel-off nail polish, New Edition, cats-would-buy-Whiskas, boogie-down, sneaking-out-to-dancehall-parties, double-dutch, Mexico, Egypt, brisket and gold necklaces, forever friends.

Thank you to the BE Book Club ladies: Amber, Delina, Demeikele, Dieula, Njoki, Tiffany, and Tricia, for curating a space of honesty, of laughter, of reflection, and of worship. Y'all are so sharp! Delina, special thanks to you for your keen eye. You are piercingly frank, and it's no wonder that you are a writing coach; you're great at observing what's missing, what's strong, what needs improvement.

To the group chats:

I see you, Rose and Camille! Your insights, sensitivity to the beauty and power of words, your nourishing snark, your feather-soft encouragement are a bounty of care. Plus, y'all are brilliant writers. Brilliant.

I see you, Kim and Tiffany! We're raising these babies together. We pray together, cry together, advance and retreat together. It started with Facebook messages during 2:00 a.m. nursing hour, and now we're sleeping (with hot flashes, but still). You both empower me to keep going. Our conversations are all over these pages.

Kathryn, this book exists in part because of you. Remember that text you sent about a prayer for your friend? I hope she is healing. I hope she was covered. And I hope this book is an answer to your question.

Thank you to my literary mothers. I learned the beauty of language through Toni Morrison and Maya Angelou. A wise teacher put their books in my hands when I was ten years old. I speak their words over myself whenever I want to rise in love or rise, still (which is to say, often). Where would I be without the literary cradling of these mothers, as well as Octavia Butler, Gwendolyn Brooks, Rita Dove, Nikki Giovanni, Sonia Sanchez, Lucille Clifton, bell hooks, and Audre Lorde? I continue to be inspired by literary sisters and aunties like Marcie Alvis Walker, Candice Benbow, Camille Hernandez, Dieula Previlon, Brittany Solomon, Cole Arthur Riley, Khristi Lauren Adams, Nya Abernathy, Dr. Wilda Gafney, Dr. Chanequa Walker-Barnes, and Dr. Angela N. Parker—just to name a few. Whew, Black women are gifted, okay?

To Camilla: you brought this book to vibrant life through your art. Thank you for lending your formidable gifts to this project. I cannot sing your praises loudly enough.

To the team at HarperCollins Christian Publishing: Bonnie, Kara, Rachel, and Tiffany, and to Victoria and Elisa: your warmth, expertise, and championing sharpened this work and put flesh on the bones. I am indebted to you, and grateful.

Thank you, Julie, for being my cheerleader, my trusted friend, my gingerbread sister. Your notes helped me create better work.

Kat, you have been consistent and generous in your support and guidance, your advocacy and protectiveness, your good questions, and your example. Thank you.

And, to my husband, Jonathan, and my wonderful sons—thank you: for not just picking me up when I felt worn down, but creating space, consistently, for me to struggle and labor; for offering constructive feedback or play time; for your prayers that helped me to give words to mine. I love you all so much. Thank you.

About the Author

Sharifa Stevens is a writer, poet, speaker, and singer. She is the daughter of Jamaican immigrants, was born and raised in New York, and currently resides with her family in Texas. She graduated from Columbia University in New York with a bachelor's degree in African American Studies before earning a master's in theology from Dallas Theological Seminary. Sharifa aspires to use writing as a vehicle that moves readers to intersect with the sacred and the honest. She co-authored *Only Light Can Do That: 60 Days of MLK—Devotions for Kids*, contributed to the books *Vindicating the Vixens: Revisiting Sexualized, Vilified, and Marginalized Women of the Bible*, and *Rally: Communal Prayers for Lovers of Jesus and Justice*, and collaborated with musical artist Lecrae on his book *Set Me Free*. Sharifa is married to a Renaissance man and is a mother to two lively boys.

About the Illustrator

Camilla Ru is a Zimbabwean-British illustrator and designer. Her work incorporates her African roots as well as her love of vibrant patterns and colors and her passion for connecting people through representation. She enjoys exploring various forms of creativity and welcomes inspirations from life's experiences to tell stories, expand imaginations, and inspire joy. She has had the privilege of working on various projects, from editorial work to literary work, promotional artwork, and more.